CONFRONTING
SEXUAL HARASSMENT

What Schools
and Colleges
Can Do

CONFRONTING SEXUAL HARASSMENT

What Schools and Colleges Can Do

JUDITH BERMAN BRANDENBURG

Teachers College, Columbia University
New York and London

Published by Teachers College Press, 1234 Amsterdam Avenue, New York, NY 10027

Library of Congress Cataloging-in-Publication Data

Brandenburg, Judith Berman.
  Confronting sexual harassment : what schools and colleges can do /
Judith Berman Brandenburg.
     p.   cm.
  Includes bibliographical references and index.
    ISBN 0-8077-3591-4 (cloth). — ISBN 0-8077-3590-6 (pbk.)
    1. Sexual harassment in education—United States.   2. Sexual
harassment in universities and colleges—United States.   3. Sexual
harassment—United States—Prevention.   I. Title.
  LC212.82.B73   1997
  379.2′6—DC21   96-44488

ISBN 0-8077-3590-6 (paper)
ISBN 0-8077-3591-4 (cloth)

Printed on acid-free paper
Manufactured in the United States of America

04 03 02 01 00 99 98 97   8 7 6 5 4 3 2 1

To the late:

A. Harry Passow
Jacob H. Schiff Professor Emeritus of Education at
Teachers College, Columbia University

and

Horace D. Taft
Professor of Physics and former Dean of Yale College,
Yale University

Two people from very different places who taught me most
about principles, justice, and care

Contents

Preface   xi

Acknowledgments   xii

Introduction   xiii

1. **Defining the Problem and Its Scope**   1

   Definitions   1

   Quid Pro Quo Harassment   2
   Hostile Environment Harassment   3
   The Issue of Repetition   4
   The Issue of Power   5
   Peer Harassment and Contrapower Harassment   6
   *Forms of Harassment That Are Inconsistently Included
     in the Definition of Sexual Harassment*   7

   Incidence of Sexual Harassment   11

   Conclusion   18

2. **Legal Responsibilities of Educational Institutions**   20

   Federal Laws Covering Sexual Harassment   21

   *Equal Protection Clause of the 14th Amendment to the
     United States Constitution*   21
   Title VII of the Civil Rights Act of 1964   22
   Title IX of the Education Amendments of 1972   23

   Important Cases and Administrative Proceedings   24

   Extent of School Responsibility   24
   Hostile Environment   28
   Peer Harassment   29
   Same-Sex Peer Harassment   32

Off-Campus Programs and Activities   33
Cases and Proceedings (Off Campus)   36
Conclusion   37

3. Origins of Sexual Harassment   **39**
Theories   40
Impact of Family and Community   42
Impact of Schools   43
Race and Ethnicity   45
Sexual Orientation   46
Conclusion   47

4. Creating Policies and Grievance Procedures   **49**
Policies   51
Consensual Relationships   52
Grievance Procedures   52
Models   53
Stages of the Grievance Procedure   55
Components of an Effective Grievance Procedure   56
Difficult Dilemmas   57
False Accusations   62
Off-Campus Programs and Activities   63
Conclusion   65

5. Educating to Raise Awareness   **66**
A Model Environment   67
Implementing Educational Strategies to Change Attitudes
    and Behavior   68
Components of an Educational Intervention on
    Sexual Harassment   71
Workshops and Presentations on Sexual Harassment   72
Case Studies for Educating to Prevent Sexual Harassment   73
Pre-Kindergarten   74
K–12 Cases   74
Higher Education Cases   78

Suggestions for Case Study Development   81
Conclusion   82

6. **Developing Educational Strategies**   83
    Higher Education   83
    Schools of Education   86
        Preparing Educational Leaders   *86*
        Working with Other Institutions   *91*
    Middle and High School Levels   92
    Early and Elementary School Levels   94
    Considerations for Parent Education   95
    Conclusion   96

**Conclusions: Frequently Asked Questions About Sexual
Harassment and Schools**   97

**Appendix A: Current State, Local, and Institutional Policies
and Grievance Procedures on Sexual Harassment**   103

**Appendix B: Educational Resources – Organizations,
Publications, Programs, and Curricular and Media Materials**   127

**Appendix C: Federal Organizations and Selected Laws Related
to Sexual Harassment and Schools**   147

References   155

Index   167

About the Author   174

Preface

Work on the difficult and complex issue of sexual harassment is still evolving. The ethical, legal, psychological, and educational implications of this issue are substantial. It may be helpful for the reader to have an idea of some of the experiences that have influenced my perspective on this issue and that inform this book.

As a psychologist, teacher, and administrator, I have worked on the issue of sexual harassment for more than 19 years. In 1977 as Associate Dean of Yale College, Yale University, I chaired a committee that established grievance procedures for sexual harassment complaints and then served for 6 years as convenor of the grievance board established to receive these complaints. Since 1985 as Professor of Psychology and Education, and for almost a decade as Dean, at Teachers College, Columbia University, I have extended my focus on sexual harassment to include elementary and secondary schools and what schools at all levels can do to stop sexual harassment.

I have had the benefit of ongoing legal consultation starting as a newly appointed associate dean who began work at Yale in the midst of the university's sexual harassment lawsuit. Most recently I have sought advice about school responsibility for preventing sexual harassment in off-campus programs and activities. I have learned much from these consultations and from the academic colleagues in a wide variety of educational institutions who have joined in considering the complicated issues associated with sexual harassment. I have been educated by the many students it has been my privilege to know. Through shared study and collaboration, including the course I developed on the "Psychology of the Undergraduate," my insight has grown.

During this period I also have profited from participation in a number of professional activities. These include my work as a member of the Visiting Committee on Undergraduate Education for the Massachusetts Institute of Technology and as a Trustee of Cornell University.

Following my experiences at Yale, I believed that clear policies and strong grievance procedures would end sexual harassment. While these measures are essential, it is clear they are not sufficient. This book explores the persistence of sexual harassment and what schools can do to address and prevent this behavior.

Acknowledgments

I acknowledge with great appreciation the contributions of many colleagues, students, teachers, administrators, and those who have been involved in sexual harassment complaints who trusted me with their experiences and views, and who have influenced my thinking and this book.

To Yale College, Yale University, where I was introduced to work on the problem of sexual harassment and saw how scholars with different perspectives passionately held could join together for the sake of truth and honor. I am forever indebted for all that I learned and for the support I received, most recently during my 1994–95 sabbatical as a Visiting Fellow in the Department of Psychology.

To Teachers College, Columbia University, for devotion to the human spirit and to education for change. My thanks to former president P. Michael Timpane for his sense of fairness and for the freedom he gave me as Dean to pursue what was important. Particular thanks go to the Council on the Scholarship on Women and Gender, to the Teacher Education Policy Committee, and to my dear colleagues in the Dean's Office.

Enormous gratitude to my outstanding research assistants, students, and friends at Teachers College, who included: in the early stages, Nina Asher and Matthew Tye for gathering information and helping with preliminary drafts; in the final stretch, Dayna Bandman for administrative support; throughout, Danielle Cimino for her care, precision, and good judgment; and most importantly, Drew LaStella for his leadership, fortitude, judgment, and for accepting my endless requests with constant good cheer. I thank Drew and Danielle for their scholarly input, and for their loyalty, support, and humor.

My appreciation to David Imig, Executive Director of the American Association of Colleges of Teacher Education, and to George Davidson, of Hughes, Hubbard & Reed, for their support and sage advice.

I thank my dear friends Harriet Spivak, Assistant Director, South Florida Employment and Training Consortium, and Myra Strober, Professor, Stanford University, for reviewing the manuscript and for providing moral support and care over the years.

To my sons, David and Neal, for their friendship and for teaching me so much that has enriched my perspective. To my husband, Lane H. Brandenburg, for his persistence in asking questions, for reviewing the manuscript, and for his endless encouragement and patience.

Introduction

Over the past few years Americans have been riveted by tales of sexual harassment in all quarters of society. We hear of incidents in the military, the workplace, the government, and the home. Unfortunately, our schools are not immune. In fact, schools may reinforce the attitudes and behaviors that underlie sexual harassment, without being aware that they are contributing to a problem. Four out of five students have experienced some form of sexual harassment in school, and 32% report being sexually harassed before seventh grade (American Association of University Women, 1993). The problem is widespread. Sexual harassment persists in spite of the publicity, known detrimental effects, and the law. Many, including some educators, continue to be unaware of its serious implications. This book is directed at assisting schools at all levels to use education, in addition to policies and grievance procedures, to address and prevent sexual harassment.

Sexual harassment involves subjecting someone to unwanted sexual attention. It includes a wide array of behavior ranging from verbal innuendo to overt sexual demands. The effects of sexual harassment can be devastating to individuals and to organizations. Sexual harassment may influence self-concept, emotional health, career path, interpersonal relationships, and the entire course of one's personal and professional life. The vulnerability of students to sexual harassment is particularly high, and its potential effects on them are severe. The threat of continued taunting, touching, and teasing by peers may cause lowered grades, physical symptoms, and truancy (AAUW, 1993; Paludi & Barickman, 1991; Shoop & Hayhow, 1994). Through fear of reprisals, a student may give in to the sexual demands of a teacher or may withdraw from a course, a major, or even a career (Crull, 1991; Gutek & Koss, 1993; Paludi & Barickman, 1991; U. S. Merit Systems Protection Board, 1981). Those sexually harassed may report physical symptoms, including insomnia, appetite disturbance, and nausea, and emotional reactions, including feelings of humiliation, anger, helplessness, and depression (Crull, 1991; Gutek & Koss, 1993; Hanisch, 1996; Shoop & Hayhow, 1994).

The entire community may be affected by the way that a school responds to sexual harassment. Third parties not directly involved in an incident of sexual harassment are affected as well. For example, when a teacher has an intimate relationship with a student, other students may hesitate to approach that teacher about academic matters, either out of discomfort or because they are concerned that they might be harassed themselves. When girls in high school hear tales of the sexual trials of other girls by a group of boys, they learn that they must always be on guard. Such experiences destroy the learning environment. The school's failure to respond effectively to sexual harassment reinforces community distrust of school policies and procedures, and of the educational enterprise.

Legally, sexual harassment is a form of sex discrimination and is an insidious barrier to equal educational opportunities for all students. Educational institutions are required by law to provide an environment free of sexual harassment. Recently the courts have awarded substantial compensatory and punitive damages to people who have been sexually harassed. Beyond monetary awards, the total cost to the educational institution in legal fees, administrative time, decreased productivity, community distrust, and loss of reputation can be enormous.

The persistence of sexual harassment in spite of the law—whether in the Navy, the federal government, or schools and universities—suggests the enduring nature of this behavior. Although a zero tolerance policy for sexual harassment was established by the Navy in 1992, sexual harassment continues. A survey of female military veterans reported that 90% had been sexually harassed, and 25% had been victims of rape or attempted rape while in the military (Murduch & Nichol, 1995). On the very day that St. John's University announced the suspension of one of its students found guilty of a brutal sexual assault on a female student by four members of a sports team, another student was raped in the St. John's gym (Fried, 1991). Instituting a sexual harassment policy and grievance procedure is necessary but not sufficient to eliminate the behavior. We must do more.

An examination of the nature of sexual harassment and why it is so difficult to eliminate suggests further action. Sexual harassment is a complex and pivotal issue rooted in fundamental attitudes, beliefs, and behaviors. An outgrowth of sex-role stereotypes, sexual harassment has come to light and may be increasing as a consequence of changes in gender roles and the distribution of power. The subjective aspect of sexual harassment adds to the confusion and the persistence. While some behaviors consistently are viewed as wrong (e.g., quid pro quo incidents of exchanging favors for sex), others are less clear. Behaviors that may be encouraged and experienced as fun by some persons are experienced as fearful and hurtful by others. How does one know?

The need to do more is suggested by the number of educators who remain unaware of the existence of sexual harassment and by others who seek assistance on this issue. Despite the high incidence of sexual harassment and the attendant publicity, knowledge of the issue among educators ranges from lack of understanding the term and failure to see why the behavior is detrimental to heightened awareness and concern. A candid respondent to a survey of educators said, "I am amazed at how little attention I have paid to the issue. I am responding to this only because you asked for a response—maybe *unaware* of this issue is a category you should include in your study" (Brandenburg, 1994b). However, another study of 11 research universities with schools of education in New York State found that all schools considered the issue of sexual harassment to be very important and that they sought assistance in addressing this problem (Brandenburg, 1994a).

I believe that the main hope for preventing sexual harassment is education. We must use education, beginning with the family and continuing from nursery school through postsecondary school, to address the attitudes, values, and behaviors that nurture sexual harassment. We as educators must examine our own attitudes and behaviors. We must continue research on sexual harassment's underlying causes and on the effectiveness of policies, grievance procedures, and educational interventions. We must identify and make public the best current practices. However, we do not have the luxury of waiting for this research to be completed. Schools are legally required to address sexual harassment now. We must take immediate steps to prohibit sexual harassment both in school and in off-campus programs and activities.

The aim of this book is to assist schools at all levels to identify sexual harassment, to respond quickly and appropriately when it occurs, and, most important, to prevent it through education. We will see how sexual harassment has been defined, what problems it causes for individuals and institutions, and what we can do about it. We will consider the psychological origins of sexual harassment that make it so intractable. I describe a multidimensional approach for schools to consider in addressing sexual harassment. I include important legal cases, sample policies and grievance procedures, a discussion of school responsibility for students in off-campus programs and activities, and case studies as examples of problems and pedagogy. I suggest aspects of systematic institutional change, educational strategies, and resources that may help to stop sexual harassment in schools.

This book attempts to raise and to clarify some of the complicated issues associated with sexual harassment. As schools and workplaces are held responsible for prohibiting and eliminating sexual harassment, they struggle to understand, to be fair, to comply with regulations, to be effective, and to sort out many competing interests and issues. The courts are still defining the extent of the institution's responsibility. When a school has effective policies and procedures and educational programs, what is the extent of its liability? What does a school do when someone who has been sexually harassed refuses to take action and asks that nothing be done? How do we balance confidentiality with a school's responsibility for a nonhostile environment? Can a school be expected to control circumstances in all its off-campus programs and activities, including those across the country and globe? Where are the boundaries between institutional and individual responsibility? Is it reasonable to hold an academic institution responsible for the acts of all members of its community (e.g., student to student harassment, faculty to student harassment)? Is the growing effort of some institutions to place legal liability on individuals accused of sexual harassment even before they are known to be guilty a reasonable one? How can an institution expect a sense of community and loyalty if it fails to support a member accused of sexual harassment in the course of fulfilling professional duties? What are appropriate limits of responsibility?

The issues of community versus individual responsibility have further implications. Rules prohibiting sexual harassment should serve the community as well as the individual. However, sometimes these rules go too far. When these rules or policies encroach on freedom of speech and academic freedom, they do a disservice to our institutions of learning. It is sometimes unclear where to draw the line. While common sense and good judgment serve us well, each instance is different and may raise difficult concerns. Sexual harassment touches on very intimate and personal behavior. How far can or should institutions go in legislating private behavior? Are expectations about faculty and staff not having dual relationships with students always clear and appropriate? How do such rules square with freedom of choice and the individual's right to privacy? What about circumstances involving students who are older than teachers? Colleagues? People who share similar role status?

We must use education to make change, mindful of the psychological implications of our efforts. In particular, as young women raise the issue of sexual harassment and demand their rights, we must find ways to support them without succumbing to the possibility, as Katie Roiphe (1993) has pointed out, of victimizing them through overprotection. The time has come when our exploration of the dynamics of sexual harassment must include consideration of the responsibility of the person harassed as well as the harasser. This must be done while showing respect for the survivor without blaming the victim. Educators and counselors must be prepared to understand and to address the issues involved in proactive and responsive ways.

Some complain that too much attention to sexual harassment is destroying male–female relationships and eliminating spontaneity in personal and professional interactions. This period of societal transition may require heightened awareness and self-consciousness in the way we relate to each other. However, such efforts eventually should foster increased communication, respect, and equality, which result in improved interactions and relationships among people and which further educational and professional opportunities.

I hope the book will be helpful to teachers, counselors, administrators, students, and parents in K–12 schools and institutions of higher education. Of course, each institution will have its own requirements and will understand the issues and use the resources in its own context. In particular, I strongly advise readers to consult their own legal counsel and the particular requirements of their state and local authorities.

CHAPTER 1

Defining the Problem and Its Scope

Only after we understand the nature of sexual harassment can we develop ways to prevent it in the future. The first step in eliminating sexual harassment is to clarify its meaning. In this chapter I map out some common ground in the definitions of sexual harassment, identify behaviors that typically are called harassing, and discuss the incidence of sexual harassment.

DEFINITIONS

Sexual harassment may be defined as unwanted sexual attention that would be offensive to a reasonable person and that negatively affects the work or school environment. The critical element in almost all definitions of sexual harassment is unwanted sexual attention. Sexual harassment includes a wide range of behaviors from verbal innuendo and subtle suggestions, to overt demands and abuse, including rape and child sexual abuse. Unfortunately, definitions of sexual harassment and their concomitant behaviors vary throughout the literature, policies, and procedures. Several categories of behavior, including gender harassment, harassment based on sexual orientation, and sexual abuse, are sometimes included under the general definition of sexual harassment and sometimes considered separately. According to the New York State Governor's Task Force on Sexual Harassment (NYSGTF), "No single definition of sexual harassment can be meaningful for all situations, purposes and individuals" (1993, p. 27). However, even as the courts continue to clarify the nature of sexual harassment, educational institutions are well advised to follow the Office for Civil Rights (OCR) and the Equal Employment Opportunity Commission (EEOC) definitions of sexual harassment and to be in compliance with Title IX of the Education Amendments of 1972 and Title VII of the Civil Rights Act of 1964. These regulations apply to educational settings since schools are places of employment and recipients of federal funds. Title IX covers behaviors that range from gender harassment to sexual assault. The definitions presented below serve as the basis for discussion throughout this book.

According to the OCR (1981):

> Sexual harassment consists of verbal or physical conduct of a sexual nature, imposed on the basis of sex, by an employee or agent of a recipient that denies, limits, provides different, or conditions the provision of aid, benefits, services or treatment protected by Title IX. (p. 2)

According to the EEOC (1980):

> Unwelcome sexual advances, requests for sexual favors, and other verbal or physical conduct of a sexual nature constitute sexual harassment when
> (1) submission to such conduct is made either explicitly or implicitly a term or condition of an individual's employment,
> (2) submission to or rejection of such conduct by an individual is used as the basis for employment decisions affecting such individual, or
> (3) such conduct has the purpose or effect of unreasonably interfering with an individual's work performance or creating an intimidating, hostile, or offensive working environment. (29 C.F.R. § 1604.11)

The EEOC (1990) describes two categories of sexual harassment, "quid pro quo" [(1) & (2) above] and "hostile environment" [(3) above].

Quid Pro Quo Harassment

Quid pro quo harassment "occurs when submission to or rejection of such [unwelcome sexual] conduct by an individual is used as the basis for employment decisions affecting such individual" (p. 2). Sexual favors or demands may be made a condition of receiving benefits (e.g., a job, promotion, grade, recommendation, or appointment) or of avoiding a penalty (e.g., being fired or receiving a negative evaluation). This category of sexual harassment often involves a power relationship such as that between a supervisor and an employee or between a teacher and a student. Examples include:

- An advisor suggests to his advisee that a positive recommendation would follow their spending a weekend together.
- A department chair offers a faculty member a preferred teaching assignment contingent on sexual favors.

- A senior is told by the tennis coach that he will not make the team if he doesn't agree to pose for nude photographs.
- A supervisor threatens to cut an employee's hours if she does not have a sexual relationship with him.

Hostile Environment Harassment

Hostile environment harassment applies when unwelcome sexual conduct causes the environment to become hostile, intimidating, or offensive, and unreasonably interferes with an employee's or student's work. The EEOC (1990) recognizes that this category of sexual harassment "can constitute sex discrimination, even if it leads to no tangible or economic job consequences" (p. 2). This form of harassment may occur between people of equal status, including students. The environment may be affected by one egregious instance of sexual harassment or by a pattern of offenses. Although this category is the more frequent form of harassment, it is often difficult for institutions to identify. Examples include

- A professor occasionally shows slides of nude women in his lectures on organic chemistry.
- Male high school students use nude pictures and sexual nicknames to decorate a lounge used by other students and teachers.
- Several co-workers in a shared office pepper their conversations and messages with sexually explicit language.
- Sexually explicit material is sent to all students on the Internet.

Generally, there is agreement as to what constitutes the most blatant forms of sexual harassment, yet viewpoints often differ regarding more subtle circumstances. The social interaction is frequently very complicated and may invite different interpretations. Whether behavior is considered sexual harassment depends to some extent on the subjective experience of the recipient. The same behavior might be enjoyed by one recipient and unwanted by another. This subjective aspect contributes to the possibility of misunderstanding and miscommunication. It would be far simpler if we could just make a list of behaviors that were prohibited (considered to be sexual harassment) in all circumstances. The courts are trying to clarify the definition of sexual harassment so that it is less subjective by applying a "reasonable person" or "reasonable woman" standard. However, any attempt to list and to legislate against whole classes of behaviors raises issues of individuals' rights and freedoms. Policies and procedures that are based on vague definitions of sexual harassment risk impinging on freedom of speech and academic freedom.

The Issue of Repetition

Ambiguity in definition contributes to questions about the significance of repetition of behavior in defining sexual harassment. Must a behavior be repeated or persistent to qualify as sexual harassment? This question touches on a number of subtleties and difficulties in establishing a shared understanding of sexual harassment and the people involved.

According to the dictionary, the term *harassment* is derived from the verb harass: "1. To irritate or torment persistently. 2. To wear out; exhaust" (*American Heritage Dictionary*, 1992). "1. To trouble, worry or torment as with cares, debts, repeated questions, etc. 2. To trouble by repeated raids or attacks" (*Webster's New World Dictionary*, 1974). The word *harass* is from the Old French word "harer: To set a dog on" (*Webster's New World Dictionary*, 1974). The Old French definition certainly captures in the vernacular what some would call the essence of sexual harassment.

These definitions contain an element of repeated activity. However, a single occurrence that is intense or dramatic also may be irritating and tormenting. Thus a single instance such as rape, a sexual approach that is particularly crude and hostile, or a clear quid pro quo offer, "If you sleep with me I will give you an A," may readily be seen as sexual harassment.

A more difficult question is: When is once not enough? When does behavior become sexual harassment only if it is repeated? In what circumstances may attention, even if unwanted, be attributed to social awkwardness, clumsy social advances, insecurity, or testing romantic interest, rather than sexual harassment? How do we account for individual differences that depend on the circumstances and the past experience of the recipient? One recipient may fend off the attention or be flattered, while another may find even one instance enormously disturbing (for example, the great distress of a young female student at being hugged by a member of the College Ministry resulted in part from her prior experience and the fact that she was a rape survivor).

The introduction to this book describes the serious consequences (emotional, social, academic, vocational, and financial) that may befall the person who is sexually harassed. Without demeaning the experience of the person being harassed, it is also important to understand the circumstances of the person accused of harassment. Should there be any difference in the way we regard the person whose behavior, while experienced as unwanted and harassing, honestly is misguided rather than intentional (for example, the lonely graduate student who expresses a social interest in a female undergraduate his own age and is surprised to learn from a grievance board member that she feels threatened because he is her teaching assistant). Helen Garner (1995) takes a sensitive and sympathetic look at the experience of the person accused of sexual harassment. She suggests that "under these stories lie great chasms of self-doubt, uncertainty and fear" (p. 186). The play *Oleanna* (Mamet, 1993) also explores the power and vulnerability of both the accuser and the person accused. In some instances excessive punishment may be unfair to both parties. The person accused may receive a lasting penalty, and the person harassed may be further injured by "victimization psychology." It is important to educate ourselves to be sensitive, to make distinctions, to use reasonable judgment, to communicate clearly, and to be assertive. However, first we must develop some shared understanding, and all of this is easier said than done. The most extreme instances we describe may be clear, but there is a large area of ambiguity. As Garner (1995) suggests, "I know that between 'being made to feel uncomfortable' and 'violence against women' lies a vast range of male and female behavior. If we deny this, we enfeeble language and drain it of meaning. We insult the suffering of women who have met real violence, and we distort the subtleties of human interaction into charicatures that serve only as propaganda for war" (p. 22).

To answer the question, sexual harassment need not be repeated, but may be based on behavior that occurs only once. According to the American Psychological Association (1992), "Sexual harassment can consist of a single intense or severe act or of multiple persistent or pervasive acts" (Code of Ethics, Standard 1.11). The difficulty is sorting out the many shades of gray.

The Issue of Power

Sexual harassment is not an exclusively sexual issue but may be an exploitation of a power relationship. Like any other power struggle, many instances of sexual harassment are initiated and negotiated by a person in a position of authority and are sustained at the expense of another who cannot counter demands without risk of reprisal (student teacher vs. student, principal vs. teacher) (Bogart & Stein, 1987; Paludi, 1990; Siegel, 1991). Sexual harassment often is experienced as a hostile act that may be intended to disempower and subjugate the person harassed. Evidence suggests that individuals employed in nontraditional work settings for their gender are somewhat more likely to be harassed (Gutek, 1985; USMSPB, 1981), and "that some men may be using sex as a way of retaliating against women at work" (Gutek, 1985, p. 119).

The largest monetary settlement obtained by the EEOC was concluded on behalf of 15 female employees who brought a sexual harassment complaint against the CEO of Del Laboratories, of Long Island, New York. The basis of the complaint was the hostile environment created by the CEO's behavior. The element of power was emphasized by the lawyer in the case, Robert Lipman, who said, "I think what the case shows us is that sexual harassment is about power and the abuse of power because of sex" (Goldberg, 1995b, p. D8).

The power component associated with sexual harassment is acknowledged by most researchers (Benson & Thomson, 1982; Paludi, 1990; Tangri & Hayes, in press; Zalk, 1990). An understanding of the power issue informs many definitions of sexual harassment. Tangri and Hayes (1996) present a careful analysis of numerous theories that attempt to explain the power component of sexual harassment based on organizational, biological, and sociocultural factors. Some striking aspects that consistently appear in these theories include gender differences where males as compared with females: (1) have greater propensity for sexuality and aggression, (2) experience a potential threat from females, especially given the number of women entering new areas of the workplace, and (3) are less sensitive to behavior that is experienced as threatening or offensive. Tannen (1994) observes the connection between power and sexual harassment by concluding that "sex entails power in our culture" (p. 257). She suggests that females routinely experience men as "intimidating," given their typically greater physical strength and positions of greater authority. She indicates that sexual harassment is used in the workplace to negotiate power.

These gender differences suggest why males are more likely than females to initiate sexual attention that may be unwanted. They provide ample basis for situations where a male fails to see the negative impact of his behavior and is confused when a female experiences that behavior as unwanted sexual attention or sexual harassment. However, power-based theories do not explain all instances of sexual harassment. In particular, the power dynamic is not always involved and not every instance of sexual harassment involves men harassing women.

Peer Harassment and Contrapower Harassment

Sexual harassment also can occur between colleagues of equal power or status (peer harassment) and when a subordinate harasses a superior (contrapower harassment) (Benson, 1984). *Peer harassment* occurs between persons of equal status or power (student vs. student and teacher vs. teacher) and is the most frequent form of sexual harassment in school settings. Some examples of peer harassment include

- A group of high school boys calling out ratings of girls as they pass by.
- A girl on the school bus making sexually charged comments to a boy while suggestively touching herself.
- A group of high school boys circulating a "Slam Book" listing students' names with derogatory sexual comments written about them by other students.
- A group of girls stripping another girl and calling her sexual names.

Contrapower harassment occurs when a subordinate in a lower-status role (with apparently little authority) harasses a person in a higher-status position (student vs. teacher). A student may assert power against a teacher or administrator by threatening to bring a sexual harassment complaint. Accusations of sexual harassment that are made public, whether authentic or false, may have a lasting negative impact on all parties irrespective of the findings. It is also possible that someone in a position of low status may intentionally use sexuality to attract and win favors from someone in authority. Some examples of contrapower harassment include

- A student trying to seduce her college advisor.
- A high school tennis star sending intimate letters to the tennis coach.
- A client repeatedly asking out his counselor.

Forms of Harassment That Are Inconsistently Included in the Definition of Sexual Harassment

The preceding examples of sexual harassment include behaviors involving unwanted sexual attention. However, broader definitions of sexual harassment also may include gender harassment and harassment based on sexual orientation.

Gender harassment involves hostile and insulting attitudes and behavior based on gender and may or may not involve unwanted sexual attention (Till, 1980). Examples include:

- A teacher telling a class that "pretty girls are not good in science."
- Susan's professor directs his lectures to the men in the class. They usually sit in a group together, and you can tell where the professor focuses his eyes and directs his voice. The professor repeatedly tells jokes about women during class (Columbia College, 1993).
- A school counselor discouraging girls from applying to engineering programs.

Harassment based on sexual orientation involves hostile and insulting attitudes and behavior based on the presumed sexual orientation of the harassed (commonly referred to as "gay bashing"); it may or may not involve unwanted sexual attention. Unless this harassment involves unwanted sexual attention it is not, strictly speaking, sexual harassment. Examples of harassment based on sexual orientation include: (1) high school students calling other students "dykes" and "fags," and (2) a parent insisting that girls who want to play basketball are gay.

Discrimination based on sexual orientation is receiving much attention from students, teachers, and administrators (Eskenazi & Gallen, 1992). According to an AAUW (1993) survey 86% of elementary and secondary school students said they would be "very upset" if they were called gay or lesbian. No other form of harassment, including physical abuse, provoked as strong a negative reaction, especially among the boys. Of the students surveyed, 17% said they have been called gay or lesbian, with boys twice as likely as girls to have been targeted in this way (AAUW, 1993). Although harassment based on sexual orientation is a major problem in our schools currently, unless this behavior involves unwanted sexual attention or sexual harassment, it is not covered under Title IX or Title VII.

Massachusetts has passed a bill to outlaw discrimination against gay and lesbian students in public schools. The new state law is intended to "affirm the rights of openly gay students to many of the rituals of adolescence: to form alliances and clubs, to take a date to the prom, to participate freely in sports" (Rimer, 1993, p. A18). The bill will make it easier for students who are targets of gay harassment to bring lawsuits against their schools.

Some schools include harassment based on sexual orientation under their sexual harassment procedures. The sexual harassment grievance procedure may be the most sensitive place to receive complaints of harassment based on sexual orientation. However, in pursuing these complaints it will be important to keep clear the distinctions between sexual harassment and harassment based on sexual orientation and to be consistent with Titles IX and VII.

Examples of harassment based on sexual orientation (first 2) and sexual harassment involving same-sex individuals (second 2) are

- Mark, a gay student, lives in a four-man suite at college. Although his straight suite-mates feel free to ask their girlfriends to spend the night, Mark is ridiculed and told to move out after he invites his friend Steve to stay over (Columbia College, 1993).
- Barbara, who wants to join the men's football team, is called a lesbian.
- A female teaching assistant reportedly sends intimate notes and invitations to one of the female undergraduates in her section.
- A male supervisor pinches and propositions a male worker in the school kitchen.

Sexual assault, rape, and child sexual abuse, the most violent forms of sexual harassment, are criminal felonies that do not require that the behavior be unwanted, and are sometimes considered separately.

Sexual assault or sexual abuse refers to unwanted sexual contact that is achieved by force or violence. Legal definitions of sexual assault vary by state, and the term sometimes is used synonymously with rape and sexual abuse. An example of a definition of criminal sexual assault is: any genital, anal, or oral penetration by a part of the accused's body or by an object, using force or without the victim's consent. Sexual assault involves causing a person to engage in a sexual act through force, threat of force, or lack of consent (persons under a certain age, intoxicated, or mentally handicapped are unable to give consent). Sexual assault includes, but is not limited to, rape and child sexual abuse.

Some authors suggest that sexual harassment is a subset of sexual assault, which has a broader meaning (Bohmer & Parrot, 1993; Shakeshaft & Cohan, 1995). This book argues that sexual harassment is the broader category as it includes subtle forms of unwanted sexual attention (leers, gestures, pictures) at one end of a continuum and violent physical forms of unwanted sexual attention (sexual assault) at the other end. Consistent with the book's view is *Leija* v. *Canutillo Independent School District* (1995), a case of teacher–student sexual abuse that was brought forward as a form of sexual harassment under Title IX.

The courts and theorists will continue to refine these definitions and to establish whether the more inclusive term is sexual harassment or sexual assault. In the meantime, it is important to view these behaviors as related and based in part on a shared set of underlying dynamics.

Rape is the engagement in nonconsensual sexual intercourse due to physical force, coercion, or threat—actual or implied. Those persons who are unable to give consent due to mental incapacity (by drugs, alcohol, mental retardation) also are considered to be coerced. Although definitions vary somewhat from state to state, most have redefined the crime from "rape" to "sexual assault" and "sexual abuse" to emphasize the violence of the offenses and to broaden the range of behaviors covered (Bourque, 1989). Statistics on rape are underestimates since many crimes go unreported. According to one of the most comprehensive studies (Koss, Gidycz, & Wisniewski, 1987), "27.5% of college women reported experiencing . . . an act which met the legal definitions of rape, which includes attempts" (p. 168). Rape is a felony and may be pursued in the courts. However, in some instances students or other members of a school community prefer to bring complaints of rape to an internal grievance procedure rather than to the police. The school grievance procedure also may be invoked in addition to a court process (see Chapter 4). A full discussion on rape is beyond the scope of this book.

Child sexual abuse refers to sexual acts involving a child, typically under the age of 18, by an adult who is responsible for the child's welfare, such as a parent, guardian, legal custodian, or person acting in that role (National Center for Missing and Exploited Children, 1993). Children who are 13 or 14 are legally protected from sexual activity with anyone 3 or more years their senior. Children under the age of 13 are legally protected from all sexual activity (Haugaard & Reppucci, 1988). All states must have in effect a child abuse and neglect law providing for the reporting of these crimes under Public Law 93-247, the Child Abuse Prevention and Treatment Act of 1974. School personnel should be trained to identify and report child abuse to proper authorities. This training may be extended to include a consideration of sexual harassment.

Child sexual abuse also occurs in schools. It is difficult to calculate the incidence since many instances go unreported or are kept confidential. According to Shakeshaft and Cohan (1995), "Estimates of the number of teachers who sexually abuse students range from .04% to 5%" (p. 514). A survey of high school students found that 13.5% had had sexual intercourse with a teacher (Wishnietsky, 1991). In a much publicized instance in the New York City schools, a first-year teacher, age 33, ran off with one of his 15-year-old students, was charged with kidnapping, and might have been charged with statutory rape. In a 4-week period following his arrest, the newspapers reported seven more incidents of sexual abuse involving New York City school employees (teachers, security guard, aide) and students (Sullivan, 1995). It is not clear whether this alarming number represents an increase in the incidence or in the reporting of sexual abuse.

Depending on the age of the student, an amorous relationship between a teacher and a primary or secondary school student (if under 18) may constitute a felony. Irrespective of age, student–teacher romances "invariably are inappropriate, unacceptable and destructive. They undermine the fundamental trust needed between students and teachers," according to Ramon Cortines, then New York City Schools Chancellor (Goldberg, 1995a, p. B8). Cortines (1995) declared that "sexual relationships with students will not be tolerated and individuals at any level will be fired for engaging in that kind of activity."

INCIDENCE OF SEXUAL HARASSMENT

Gender, race, class, or position does not in itself determine who will experience sexual harassment. A study at Cornell University found that of the reported cases of sexual harassment, 90% were incidents of men harassing women, 1% were women harassing men, and 9% were same-sex cases (Parrot, 1991). In a study of sexual abuse in schools by Shakeshaft and Cohan (1995), the vast majority (96%) of the abusers were males. "Of the students the males sexually abused, 76% were female, and 24% were male. Of the students females sexually abused, 86% were female, and 14% were male" (Shakeshaft & Cohan, 1995, p. 516). In the workplace 40 to 60% of women report being sexually harassed (30 to 45% of those by someone in a supervisory position, and 55 to 70% by peers) and about 15% of men (about 6 to 25% of those by someone in a supervisory position, 75 to 94% by peers) (Gutek, 1985; NYSGTF, 1993; USMSPB, 1981 & 1988).

The present distribution of power and the dynamics of existing sex roles make it much more likely that women will be candidates for sexual harassment (Brandenburg, 1982). However, as more women assume positions of authority, it is possible that the dynamics will shift. In fact, there are some reports that male complaints of sexual harassment are increasing, although the numbers remain small (Fitzgerald, 1992). Data from the Office for Civil Rights (1994) reveal that men filed 10% of the sexual harassment complaints received between October 1989 and

November 1993. One of only a few cases involving male-on-male sexual harassment that has gone to court was brought by an employee at Independent Life and Accident Insurance Company in Jacksonville, Florida. "A man who said his male boss had grabbed his crotch and kissed him on the neck has won a lawsuit based on an accusation of male-on-male sexual harassment" ("Man Wins Harassment," 1995, p. 15). It is important to keep in mind that an instance of sexual harassment that involves a male in authority as the harasser of a female subordinate is not the only possibility.

The incidence of sexual harassment is greater in certain circumstances. Sexual harassment is associated with the presence of alcohol and participation in group residences, teams, or fraternities (Benson, Charlton, & Goodhart, 1992; Berkowitz, 1992; Matthews, 1993). In addition, incidents of sexual harassment are more likely to occur in situations that involve one-on-one relationships. The relationships that students have with a counselor, coach, music instructor, tutor, or advisor are particularly vulnerable (Shakeshaft & Cohan, 1995). Sexual harassment in the workforce is more likely in settings with an imbalance of gender ratios and particularly during the initial integration of jobs that were formerly single sexed (e.g., women in the military or fire department, men in nursing) (Fain & Anderton, 1987; Kanter, 1977; USMSPB, 1981).

Sexual harassment in schools and colleges occurs between and among individuals who are students, teachers, and other school personnel. The comprehensive study of eighth through eleventh graders by the American Association of University Women (1993) reports that 81% of all students (including 85% of girls and 76% of boys) experience sexual harassment. This percentage may seem high, but is quickly understandable given the wide range of behaviors, including hostile environment harassment, used to operationalize sexual harassment in the study. The incidence among students (often only women sampled) of harassment by teachers and other school employees most frequently has been reported as about 15 to 30% at the secondary level and 30 to 65% at the postsecondary level (Adams, Kottke, & Padgitt, 1983; AAUW, 1993; Benson & Thomson, 1982; Brown & Maestro-Scherer, 1986; Dziech & Weiner, 1990; Strauss, 1988). However, the most frequent form of sexual harassment in schools and colleges is student to student, or peer harassment, which has been reported as affecting roughly 60 to 70% of students in K–12 schools and about 75% of female students in postsecondary schools (AAUW, 1993; Brown & Maestro-Scherer, 1986). This predominant type of sexual harassment also is prohibited by Title IX.

The incidence of sexual harassment reported in the literature varies depending on the sample, the definition of sexual harassment, and the methodology used in the study. Samples that include only women report a higher incidence since sexual harassment continues to be experienced disproportionately by females. We know less about the incidence and experiences of harassment of men since males frequently are not included in research samples. When the definition is confined to forced or coerced sexual advances (including quid pro quo sexual harassment) incidence for women is generally reported to be between 15 and 50% (see, for example, Dziech & Weiner, 1990; USMSPB, 1988). When the definition includes hostile environment and less severe forms of sexual harassment (such as leers, remarks, etc.), the numbers range from 50 to 90% (Fitzgerald et al., 1988; Sandroff, 1992).

The methodology that asks survey respondents directly if they have been "sexually harassed" tends to yield lower incidence rates (between 15 and 60%) (Dey, Sax, & Korn, 1994; Sandroff, 1992) than the method that does not use the label of sexual harassment but asks respondents whether they have experienced specific types of behaviors (behavioral equivalents of sexual harassment). The behavioral equivalents that are included differ based on the researcher's definition of sexual harassment. Differential incidence rates according to method may be interpreted in several ways. In some cases, respondents unfamiliar with the term *sexual harassment* may not have known that their experiences fell within this category even though they felt harassed. In other cases, a behavior experienced once might be indicated on a survey and coded as sexual harassment even if the respondent did not feel harassed. The latter is more likely with less severe forms of sexual harassment, such as those traditionally labeled gender harassment. With these less severe forms, it may be that the behavior needs to endure or be pervasive before it is experienced as sexual harassment (Gruber, Smith, & Kauppinen-Toropainen, 1996). See Table 1.1 for a summary of selected sexual harassment studies that includes definitions, methodology, and incidence reported.

The number of sexual harassment complaints filed underreports drastically the number of incidents. It is estimated that less than 10% of those sexually harassed file complaints (National Council for Research on Women, 1992). People hesitate to bring complaints, fearing embarrassment, difficulty proving their case, lack of support from colleagues, and reprisals. While variations in available studies make a single incidence level of sexual harassment illusive, a conservative estimate is that during their college and professional lives, at least 50% of women and 14% of men will experience sexual harassment. In summary, despite differences in definitions, methodology, and samples, the conclusion of

Table 1.1 Selected Studies on Sexual Harassment: Incidence, Definitions, Methods

Study	Sample and Method	Incidence	Definition of Sexual Harassment
At Work			
United States Merit Systems Protection Board, 1981 Federal workers	n = 20,083 Women = 10,648 (53%) Men = 9,302 (47%) Survey; incidence checklist and descriptive	42% of women, 15% of men reported sexual harassment; of those harassed: 22% of men harassed by men 3% of women by women 65% of women by co-worker 37% of women by supervisor 76% of men by co-worker 14% of men by supervisor	"Deliberate or repeated unsolicited verbal comments, gestures or physical contact of a sexual nature which are unwelcome"; includes behaviors from remarks to rape
United States Merit Systems Protection Board, 1988 Federal workers	n = 8,523 Survey; incidence checklist and descriptive	42% of women, 14% of men reported sexual harassment; of those harassed: 69% of women by co-worker 29% of women by supervisor 77% of men by co-worker 19% of men by supervisor	Unwanted and uninvited sexual attention; includes behaviors from remarks to rape
Gutek, 1985 Private sector workers	n = 1,232 Women = 827 (67%) Men = 405 (33%) Phone survey; incidence checklist and descriptive	53.1% of women, 37.3% of men reported sexual harassment; of those harassed: 44.8% of women by supervisor 5.5% of men by supervisor	Not specified; includes perceptions and behaviors
New York State Governor's Task Force on Sexual Harassment, 1993 Workers	n = 84 Women = 77 (92%) Men = 7 (8%) Survey of complainants; descriptive	Complainants: 92% women 8% men Harassers: 86% men 14% women 78% supervisors 22% peers	"When sexual conduct, such as words, physical contact or the display of sexual materials, is used in a workplace or an educational institution to bully, intimidate or for other similar negative and aggressive purposes, the behavior constitutes sexual harassment."

14

Sandroff, 1992	n > 9,000 (unspecified)	60% reported sexual harassment; of those harassed:	Not specified	
Magazine readers	Magazine survey; not specified, includes open ended	83% harassed by supervisor 17% by peer or subordinate; 25% fired or left job as result		
Dey et al., 1994	n = 29,771 Women = 9,402 (32%) Men = 20,369 (68%)	15% of women, 3% of men reported being harassed at current institution	Not specified; includes a range of behaviors, and misuse of power	
College faculty	Survey; "Have you been sexually harassed at this institution?"			
In Higher Education				
Fitzgerald et al., 1988	n = 2,599 Women = 1,746 (67%) Men = 853 (33%)	Women: 50% (Univ. 1) & 76% (Univ. 2) experienced sexual harassment by faculty	Not specified; includes gender harassment, seductive behavior, sexual bribery, sexual coercion, and sexual assault	
College students, undergraduate and graduate	Survey; incidence checklist	Men: not analyzed, 36% of respondents experienced gender harassment		
Benson & Thomson, 1982	n = 269 women Survey; incidence checklist	29.7% were sexually harassed by at least one male instructor during college career	"Any unwanted sexual leers, suggestions, comments or physical contact which you find objectionable in the context of a student–teacher relationship"	
College students, undergraduate females				
Adams et al., 1983	n = 372 Women = 65% Men = 35%	65% of women, 27% of men experienced some form of sexual harassment by faculty; 13% of women and 3% of men avoided taking class	Not specified; includes behaviors from comments to bribery	
College students; undergraduate and graduate	Survey; incidence checklist			

Study	Sample and Method	Incidence	Definition of Sexual Harassment
Brown & Maestro-Scherer, 1986 College students, female	n = 786 women Survey; incidence checklist	61% experienced at least one form of sexual harassment by authority; 78% harassed by peers; 12% avoided a class	EEOC definition; includes sexist comments, unwelcome attention, body language, verbal advances, invitations, physical advances, explicit sexual propositions, sexual coercion/bribery
In K-12 Schools			
AAUW, 1993 Students, grades 8-11	n = 1,632 Survey; incidence checklist	81% of all students were sexually harassed: 85% of girls 76% of boys Of those harassed: 79% by peers 18% by school personnel	"Unwanted and unwelcome sexual behavior which interferes with your life"
Stein, Marshall, & Tropp, 1993 Students, females, age 9-19, grades 2-12	n = 2,002 *Seventeen* magazine survey; incidence checklist	89% were sexually harassed Harassers: 96% peers 4% teachers and staff 97% male 3% female	"Any form of unwanted sexual attention . . . defined by the person who is the target of the harassment"
Wishnietsky, 1991 (a) Students (as reported by superintendents)	n = 65 Survey of superintendents of North Carolina High Schools	27.7% reported applying discipline for sexual harassment during previous 3 years. Of 26 instances: 18 by male faculty of female student 4 by male faculty of male student 2 by female faculty of male student 2 by female faculty of female student	EEOC definition

Wishnietsky, 1991 (b) Students	n = 148 Female = 105 (71%) Male = 43 (29%)	90 reported instances of sexual harassment: 68 (75%) by male faculty of female student 12 (13%) by male faculty of male student 4 (4%) by female faculty of male student 6 (7%) by female faculty of female student	EEOC definition
Strauss, 1988 Students, female, age 16–18	n = 133 girls Survey; incidence checklist	About 50% were sexually harassed; 30% of those harassed by teachers	OCR; behaviors include comments to attempted rape; sexual harassment is in eye of beholder
Shakeshaft & Cohan, 1995 Students, K–12	n = 225 Interviews with superintendents, lawyers, parents, and teachers	Of those sexual abuse cases reported: 89% (92% boys, 88% girls) involved contact abuse; 38% at elementary level, 20% at middle schools, 36% at high schools	4 types of sexual abuse: Non-contact: Level 1 — visual Level 2 — verbal Contact: Level 1 — pinching, touching, etc. Level 2 — molestation and sex
Roscoe, Strouse & Goodwin, 1994 Students	n = 561 Females = 281 Males = 280 Survey; incidence checklist	50% of girls and 36.8% of boys indicated experiencing at least one form of sexual harassment by peers; most harassers male	Not specified; includes comments to sexual assault for girls, more severe for boys

Numbers do not necessarily total due to incomplete data and/or nonexclusive categories.

the vast majority of studies is that sexual harassment is a widespread problem.

CONCLUSION

Sexual harassment is a complicated issue that covers a wide range of behaviors. The elements of unwanted sexual attention and abuse of power frequently are included in a description of sexual harassment. However, these factors are not always present, and the complicated, subjective nature of the behavior makes it difficult to define sexual harassment in a way that would apply to every instance. Consequently, variations in definitions of sexual harassment exist throughout the literature. Given legal requirements, educational institutions are wise to incorporate the definitions of sexual harassment as described by the OCR and EEOC.

This book considers sexual harassment as unwanted sexual attention that would be offensive to a reasonable person and that negatively affects the work or school environment. The book defines sexual harassment according to the EEOC (1980): "Unwelcome sexual advances, requests for sexual favors, and other verbal or physical conduct of a sexual nature constitute sexual harassment when (1) submission to such conduct is made either explicitly or implicitly a term or condition of an individual's employment, (2) submission to or rejection of such conduct by an individual is used as the basis for employment decisions affecting such individual, or (3) such conduct has the purpose or effect of unreasonably interfering with an individual's work performance or creating an intimidating, hostile, or offensive working environment" (29 C.F.R. § 1604.11). This definition includes quid pro quo and hostile environment sexual harassment.

Descriptions are given in this chapter for different forms of sexual harassment, including quid pro quo, hostile environment, peer harassment, contrapower harassment, gender harassment, harassment based on sexual orientation, and the extreme forms of child sexual abuse, rape, and sexual assault. A continuum of sexual harassment behavior, all covered by Title IX, exists from the more subtle verbal manifestations to the blatant physical acts of sexual abuse. The existence of this continuum underscores the importance of addressing even the most subtle incidents of sexual harassment.

The reported incidence of sexual harassment varies depending on the sample, the definition, and the methodology. It is estimated that during their professional lives about 50% of women and 14% of men will experience sexual harassment (Gutek, 1985; USMSPB, 1981, 1988). Typically, studies of students across educational levels report that 15 to 65% experience sexual harassment by teachers and school employees, and 60 to 75% experience sexual harassment by peers (Adams et al., 1983; AAUW, 1993; Benson & Thomson, 1982; Brown & Maestro-Scherer, 1986; Strauss, 1988). The problem of sexual harassment is clearly widespread.

CHAPTER 2

Legal Responsibilities of Educational Institutions

Sexual harassment is a problem of long standing that was first labeled as it emerged as a public concern in the mid-1970s and has recently reached a level of wide public debate. The major federal laws that have been implemented pertaining to sexual harassment have stood for decades, most notably Title VII of the Civil Rights Act of 1964, which governs employment, and Title IX of the Education Amendments of 1972, which governs educational institutions. In *Cannon* v. *University of Chicago* (1979), the Supreme Court established the right of an individual to bring a private lawsuit under Title IX. *Alexander* v. *Yale University* (1980) demonstrated that a sexual harassment suit could be brought under Title IX. However, sexual harassment law under Title IX is relatively undeveloped. Although the courts are still in the process of refining the definition of sexual harassment and clarifying issues of institutional responsibility, schools increasingly have been subject to legal action and have paid damages to persons bringing sexual harassment complaints. Students have sued a community college for $6,000,000 and a university for $3,000,000 on grounds of sexual harassment (Douglas, 1993; Hoffman, 1994). The courts have held institutions responsible for employees found guilty of sexual harassment.

As the number of complaints increases, institutions fear multimillion dollar claims and the issue of institutional versus individual responsibility is heightened. In at least two instances, institutions in Virginia are attempting to avoid liability for faculty members' conduct in sexual harassment cases (Wilson, 1995). This suggests an effort to depart from current practice where institutions normally defend faculty in lawsuits concerning their professional responsibilities, at least until they are found liable. *Karibian* v. *Columbia University* (1994), a Title VII case to be described later, sets what may be an extreme standard of absolute institutional responsibility for hostile environment sexual harassment wherein a supervisor abuses authority. However, the rejection by academic institutions of any responsibility for individual faculty accused of sexual harassment in the course of professional responsibilities seems equally extreme. Both positions in the extreme are potentially devastating to the educational community and the academic enterprise.

Educational institutions are legally responsible for prohibiting sexual harassment on their campuses and in their off-campus educational programs and activities. Institutions must act to prevent both quid pro quo and hostile environment sexual harassment, as described in Chapter 1. They are responsible for the actions of employees, especially officers and supervisors. An increasing body of case law also holds them responsible for student to student, or peer, harassment. This responsibility extends to off-campus sites, including field placement and internships (*Lipsett* v. *University of Puerto Rico*, 1988; *Moire* v. *Temple University School of Medicine*, 1986; *Rosa H.* v. *San Elizario Independent School District*, 1995), and to school vehicles transporting students and school personnel (*Eden Prairie, Minnesota*, 1992).

The following sections cite the central federal statutes and regulations that prohibit sexual harassment by public entities in the workplace, higher education, and K–12 schools, and summarize a number of important legal cases and administrative procedures. These cases illustrate the development of case law in interpreting the relevant federal laws as they apply to school settings and to defining sexual harassment. The decisions of the courts addressing sexual harassment indicate that policies and grievance procedures are necessary, but do not ensure that an educational institution will not be found liable for sexual harassment. Additionally, they show that schools may be responsible for preventing sexual harassment at every level, including peer harassment, and that this responsibility can extend beyond the walls of the institution. A separate section details a school's responsibility to prohibit sexual harassment in off-campus programs and activities. Succeeding chapters (4 and 8) will discuss and illustrate how educational institutions may create sexual harassment policies and grievance procedures.

This review of sexual harassment and the law is intended as a general guide. Institutions should seek legal counsel to ensure that the policies and practices they develop comply with state and local rules as well as federal statutes, and to ensure that they are doing all that they can to prevent sexual harassment.

FEDERAL LAWS COVERING SEXUAL HARASSMENT

Equal Protection Clause of the 14th Amendment to the United States Constitution

> No State shall make or enforce any law which shall abridge the privileges or immunities of citizens of the United States; nor shall any state

deprive any person of life, liberty, or property, without due process
of law; nor deny to any person within its jurisdiction the equal protection of the laws. (U.S. Constitution, Amendment XIV, Sec. 1)

The Equal Protection Clause of the14th Amendment to the United
States Constitution, excerpted above, prohibits states from denying due
process or equal protection of the laws. Section 1983 of the Civil Rights
Act of 1871 gives citizens a right to sue a state or its subdivisions for
violations of the 14th Amendment. According to the courts, public institutions may be held liable under section 1983/the 14th Amendment
for intentional sexual harassment. Victims may seek compensatory and
punitive damages as well as injunctive relief. Few sexual harassment
suits actually have been brought under this amendment as: (1) it pertains
only to offenders acting "under color of state law" (i.e., public employees), and (2) an employer will be held liable for acts of an employee only
if a claimant can show that the harassment "was part of a pattern so
striking as to allow an inference of supervisory encouragement, condo-
nation, or acquiescence and that it caused the deprivation of rights"
(Wetherfield, 1990, p. 27).

Title VII of the Civil Rights Act of 1964

Most sexual harassment suits have been brought under Title VII of
the Civil Rights Act of 1964, which states, in part

It shall be unlawful employment practice for an employer
(1) to fail or refuse to hire or to discharge any individual, or other-
     wise to discriminate against any individual with respect to his
     compensation, terms, conditions, or privileges of employment,
     because of such individual's race, color, religion, sex, or national
     origin; or
(2) to limit, segregate or classify his employees or applicants for
     employment in any way which would deprive or tend to deprive
     any individual of employment opportunities or otherwise ad-
     versely affect his status as an employee, because of such individu-
     al's race, color, religion, sex, or national origin. (42 U.S.C. §
     2000e-2(a))

Although Title VII does not specifically discuss sexual harassment,
the phrase "terms, conditions, or privileges of employment" has been
interpreted since the late 1970s to include the psychological, as well
as physical and economic, environment. In 1986, the Supreme Court

approved this interpretation in *Meritor Savings Bank* v. *Vinson* (discussed later).

The Equal Employment Opportunity Commission, the body charged with enforcing Title VII, established the most widely used definition of sexual harassment in its *Guidelines on Discrimination Because of Sex* (EEOC, 1980). Under this definition, both quid pro quo sexual harassment and hostile environment sexual harassment are recognized, as discussed in Chapter 1. These guidelines also established institutional liability for acts of supervisors and employees. Under the Civil Rights Act of 1991, the harassed may seek both compensatory and punitive damages for violations of Title VII.

Title IX of the Education Amendments of 1972

Sexual harassment in education and educational institutions is prohibited under Title IX of the Education Amendments of 1972, which states

> No person in the United States shall, on the basis of sex, be excluded from participation in, be denied the benefits of, or be subjected to discrimination under any education program or activity receiving Federal financial assistance. (20 U.S.C. § 1681(a))

The Supreme Court established an individual's right to file a private lawsuit under Title IX in *Cannon* v. *University of Chicago* (1979). Currently, individuals can seek compensatory and injunctive relief from an institution. Between 1984 and 1987, Title IX was narrowly defined to cover only specific departments and programs that directly received federal funds. The Civil Rights Restoration Act of 1987 established that protection under Title IX applies to all parts of any institution receiving any type of federal funds. Interpretations and precedents established under Title VII, including the right of individual students to bring suit, have been applied to Title IX. Title IX is enforced by the Office for Civil Rights of the United States Department of Education.

Title IX requires that recipients (educational institutions that receive federal funds) adopt and publish grievance procedures for handling complaints of sexual harassment. Specifically, Department of Education regulations provide that

> (a) *Designation of responsible employee.* Each recipient shall designate at least one employee to coordinate its efforts to comply with and carry out its responsibilities under this [regulation], including any

investigation of any complaint communicated to such recipient alleging its noncompliance with this [regulation] or alleging any actions which would be prohibited by this [regulation]. The recipient shall notify all its students and employees of the name, office address and telephone number of the employee or the employees appointed pursuant to this paragraph.

(b) Complaint procedure of recipient. A recipient shall adopt and publish grievance procedures providing for prompt and equitable resolution of student and employee complaints alleging any action which would be prohibited by this [regulation]. (34 C.F.R. § 106(8)(a)(b))

IMPORTANT CASES AND ADMINISTRATIVE PROCEEDINGS

The following cases and administrative proceedings have important implications for understanding the legal responsibilities of educational institutions with respect to sexual harassment. I have grouped the cases in four categories: (1) extent of school responsibility, (2) hostile environment, (3) peer harassment, and (4) off-campus programs and activities. However, these categories are not mutually exclusive and often cases have multiple implications beyond the designated categories, which also are indicated.

Extent of School Responsibility

Alexander v. *Yale University* (1980) was the first sexual harassment suit to be brought under Title IX. In this case, five students brought suit against the university for what they claimed was a failure to seriously consider and investigate complaints of sexual harassment. While the court found for Yale, the decision is an important precedent for several reasons. For example, the court determined for the first time that a student's claim that she received a low grade for refusing to submit to sexual demands could be stated under Title IX, and hence set the precedent for sexual harassment suits under Title IX. However, the claim by other students that a "hostile environment" was created by the professor's actions combined with the university's lack of a grievance procedure was dismissed as not falling under the jurisdiction of Title IX. Later, in *Moire* v. *Temple University School of Medicine* (1986), the court for the first time acknowledged that the EEOC Guidelines on Sexual Harassment, which recognize a hostile or offensive environment as sexual harassment, are applicable under Title IX. (This case is described later in the section on off-campus programs and activities.)

Korf v. *Ball State* (1984) was an important early case regarding the responsibilities of faculty to their students. In this case, a professor brought a Constitutional challenge under Section 1983 in relation to his dismissal for having made sexual advances toward male students, on the grounds that he did not have adequate warning since his was the first such dismissal. The court upheld the dismissal, claiming that "common sense, reason and good judgment" adequately warned him. Further, the court intimated that a student's consent to a relationship was irrelevant when the charge was that the professor was "exploiting students for his private advantage." The dismissal was upheld in spite of the fact that the college had no policy on sexual harassment. In this case, the court allowed the use of the American Association of University Professors (AAUP) ethics statement about a professor's "proper role as an intellectual guide and counselor" to stand as a university policy (Educators Guide to Controlling Sexual Harassment [EGCSH], 1993, Appendix C, p. 55). While in this case AAUP guidelines were allowed to serve as a policy, it is important to reiterate that schools are required under Title IX to have a grievance procedure. Without such policies and procedures for sexual harassment, schools are vulnerable to accusations of hostile environment.

Stoneking v. *Bradford Area School District* (1992), which set a precedent for a district's guilt by inaction, is one of the most important cases for K–12 schools. In this case, a student brought suit under Section 1983, alleging that a public school band director used force, threats, intimidation, and coercion to sexually abuse and harass her. Further, the student claimed that the school authorities were aware of it but failed to take action. The court found that the school could be held liable because its inaction constituted an official custom and practice of reckless or deliberate indifference.

Franklin v. *Gwinnett County Public Schools* (1992) is a Supreme Court decision holding that a student may seek monetary damages from a school under Title IX, establishing a major precedent. In this case, a high school student sued her school district for sexual harassment by a teacher that had occurred over several years, including forcible kissing, sexual conversations, telephone calls, and forced intercourse in the teacher's office. As in *Stoneking*, she charged that the school district was aware and did nothing, that she was discouraged from pressing charges, and also that the district had no formal policy or procedure for sexual harassment complaints.

In *Doe* v. *Petaluma City School District* (1993), the district court first held that student-to-student sexual harassment is actionable under Title IX. This case has further implications regarding the responsibility of school employees, and in delimiting individual versus institutional responsibility. A girl sued her school district and a school counselor under Title IX and Section 1983 and sought damages because she was the subject of ongoing verbal, and occasionally physical, sexual harassment, which the school failed to stop although the girl's counselor was repeatedly notified of the situation. Although much of the case initially was dismissed, the judge did allow that the plaintiff could seek damages from the school under Title IX if she could prove that school officials intentionally failed to stop the harassment. On May 12, 1995, the Court of Appeals for the Ninth Circuit reversed a district court decision denying qualified immunity to the counselor since at the time (1990–1992) it had not been clearly established that a counselor had a duty under Title IX to prevent sexual harassment by peers. Thus the school district will be the sole defendant when the case is tried. This decision may be influential as a series of cases dealing with individual versus institutional liability are filed in the future (as discussed later). It identifies the date of the harassment relative to the existing legal interpretation of Title IX as an important factor in deciding liability (EGCSH, 1993).

Karibian v. *Columbia* (1994) is a $3,000,000 suit under Title VII and Title IX by a former Columbia student and employee against the university for quid pro quo and hostile environment sexual harassment. The case is now concluded but may be appealed. Although the case may be appealed, a decision by the Court of Appeals for the Second Circuit has established the principle that employers are absolutely liable where their employee supervisors abuse their delegated authority by creating a hostile work environment. It also could make claims of quid pro quo sexual harassment much easier to prove.

The student claims that while she worked as an employee in the university's Development and Alumni Relations Office, her supervisor forced her into a violent sexual relationship and altered her raises, hours, and other conditions of employment according to how she responded to his advances. (She had been promoted and had received raises during her relationship with the supervisor.) In November 1993, a Federal District Court ruled that Columbia could not be held liable for quid pro quo harassment since the employee could not prove economic loss, and could not be liable for the supervisor's creation of a hostile environment because Columbia provided a reasonable avenue for making complaints and acted promptly to cure the harassment once it received notice. In January 1994, the U.S. Court of Appeals for the Second Circuit reversed this decision, stating that a victim of sexual harassment does not need to prove actual harm since "such a rule would only encourage harassers to increase their persistence." To require proof of actual harm would punish those who have advanced by succumbing to harassment and encourage harassing tactics short of a pay cut or firing. With regard to Columbia's liability for the supervisor's creating a hostile work environment, the Second Circuit held that "an employer is liable for the discriminatorily abusive work environment created by a supervisor if the supervisor uses his actual or apparent authority to further the harassment." The Supreme Court declined Columbia's request to review the appeals court ruling. On February 13, 1996 a federal court jury awarded Karibian damages of $450,000, but did not find sexual harassment ("Columbia Loses Harassment Suit," 1996). However, the judge held that since there was no sexual harassment, there was no cause of action and no damages were awarded. The case may still be appealed.

Employers already were legally responsible for quid pro quo harassment by their employee supervisors. Under *Karibian* they also are absolutely liable for the actions of their supervisors to a greater degree than previously. Essentially, an employer may be held liable even if it has effective policies and procedures for hearing complaints, even if the person bringing claim failed to use them, and even if the employer could not be reasonably expected to have known of the harassment.

Two cases, not yet tried, illustrate what may become a trend of educational institutions asserting that individual faculty members are solely liable for sexually harassing behavior. A student has sued the College of William and Mary for failing to address her allegations of sexual harassment by a professor, claiming that she received a poor grade for rebuffing his sexual advances. The college has filed a complaint in federal court against the professor, claiming that he should pay damages should he be found guilty since the college has prohibited sexual harassment and the professor failed to follow the rules and "had a duty to act in ways that did not expose the college, his employer, to liability" (Wilson, 1995, p. A20).

In a similar case, *Kadiki* v. *Virginia Commonwealth University* (1995), a woman student sued the university under Title IX for failure to address an incident of sexual harassment as such. The professor was found guilty of assault and battery for the incident in which he spanked the student for doing poorly on an exam and threatened to spank her again if she did not do better upon retaking the exam. Although the college did not address the charge under its sexual harassment policy, the court dismissed the student's claim of hostile environment harassment as the college took "prompt and remedial action" and imposed sanctions on the professor. However, the court allowed the student's claim of quid pro quo sexual harassment to proceed to trial because from the facts a jury could conclude that the professor's conduct regarding re-examination was an incident of sexual harassment. The court stated that if the professor was found guilty of quid pro quo harassment, the university would be held strictly liable.

Another case underscores the school district's strict liability for the acts of the teacher and considers child sexual abuse as a form of sexual harassment protected by Title IX. In *Leija* v. *Canutillo Independent School District* (1995), the court held that in a teacher–student sexual abuse case under Title IX, the school district is strictly liable for the acts of the teacher. The court limited the damages in a Title IX teacher–student sexual abuse case to expenses for medical treatment, mental health treatment, and special education. In this case a second-grade female student allegedly was sexually abused by her physical education teacher throughout a school year. The girl told her primary teacher about the abuse and was ignored; when the parents confronted the teacher, she convinced them that nothing was happening and continued to take no action. The court remanded for retrial the issue of damages.

Hostile Environment

Bundy v. *Jackson* (1981) was an important case that supported the notion of "environmental harassment" and the premise that a hostile work environment could constitute sexual harassment. In this case, a female plaintiff claimed that subjecting employees to sexual harassment was a violation of Title VII, even if no "tangible" loss or direct employment consequences occurred. The court agreed: It was the first time a court recognized that sexual harassment was actionable for reasons other than job harm, such as discharge or failure to promote (Woerner & Oswald, 1993).

Meritor Savings Bank v. *Vinson* (1986) was the first Supreme Court ruling on sexual harassment that considered the issues of hostile environment and employer liability. The suit was brought under Title VII by a female bank employee against her supervisor and the bank in which she worked. Her claim was that she submitted to the sexual demands of her supervisor for fear that refusal would threaten her job. The case was tried several times, successively being remanded to higher courts. Eventually the Supreme Court agreed that the case should be considered under the "hostile environment" condition established by the EEOC in its guidelines. Perhaps most significantly, the court also established that the appropriate inquiry in cases of sexual harassment is whether the victim indicated that sexual advances were unwelcome, not whether the harassed voluntarily consented to sexual relations. The court also held that while employers are not automatically liable for sexual harassment, they may be liable depending on the circumstances.

Harris v. *Forklift Systems, Inc.* (1993) was the Supreme Court's second sexual harassment case under Title VII. The case involved a woman employee who claimed to be the subject of repeated sexual innuendo and demeaning comments from the company's president. A lower court that first heard the case found for the company since there was no evidence that the comments affected the woman employee's psychological well-being. The Supreme Court rejected the need to produce evidence of psychological harm to the victim. The Court held that the law is broken whenever "the environment would reasonably be perceived, and is perceived, as hostile or abusive." In the words of Justice O'Connor, the protection of federal law "comes into play before the harassing conduct leads to a nervous breakdown" (Greenhouse, 1993, pp. A1, 22). This decision seems to make it easier to bring a successful suit on the grounds of sexual harassment.

The OCR ruling in *Newark Unified School District* (1993) illustrates that schools must be conscientious about incidents that may be sexual harassment and create a hostile environment. The offending incident in this case was an ongoing "Friday Flip-up Day" game, in which boys (first through third grade) flipped up girls' dresses. The OCR found that the district failed to ensure a nondiscriminatory educational environment in permitting this for more than 5 years.

Howard v. *Board of Education of Sycamore Community Unit School District # 427* (1995) is a case that includes contrapower harassment in which a public school teacher claimed that she was sexually harassed both by fellow teachers and students. The court held that the comprehensive provisions of Title VII preclude an educational institution employee from bringing a private cause of action for gender discrimination under Title IX. A teacher's remedy is therefore under Title VII, not Title IX. Regarding the students' harassment of the teacher, the court held that a principal, who intentionally permits students to sexually harass a teacher after the teacher has given the principal notice of the harassment, deprives the teacher of equal protection and may be sued under Section 1983. The official is not protected by qualified immunity merely because students, who are subordinates, rather than supervisors or fellow teachers were harassing the teacher.

Peer Harassment

Eden Prairie, Minnesota (1992) (also known as *Mutziger* v. *Independent School District #272*, 1992, the Minnesota Department of Human Rights filing of the case) has gained much attention as a result of the ages of the children involved, the fact that the harassment occurred off school property, and the fact that the school was held responsible for preventing student to student sexual harassment. The mother of a 7-year-old second grader filed state and federal charges against her school district for sexual harassment. On the school bus, several boys teased the girl and her friends on a continuing basis, including calling them "bitches" and taunting them for having "stinky vaginas." The mother complained to the school and the district verbally and in writing repeatedly, and eventually two boys were disciplined and taken off the bus. While the settlement in the case is still pending, the United States Department of Education ruled that the district violated federal law by "failing to take timely and effective responsive action to address . . . multiple or severe acts of sexual harassment." Although the district did eventually take action by removing the offending boys from the bus, and although they did have written policies and procedures for dealing with sexual harassment, they failed to identify these incidents as sexual harassment and to follow their own procedures. This was the first federal finding establishing the elementary school's responsibility to prevent student to student sexual harassment (Eaton, 1993; EGCSH, 1993).

There have been a number of suits based on similar allegations, and many more in progress. In San Francisco (1992), a school district settled with a student for $20,000 for its failure to check verbal harassment from other students. In Minnesota (1992), a student received a $15,000 settlement for "mental anguish" from a school district that failed to remove obscene graffiti about her from a bathroom (*Lyle* v. *Independent School District #709*, 1991). In Illinois (1992), a third-grade girl filed suit against her school district for allowing a boy to pinch her chest, groin, and buttocks from first through third grade. She has moved to a private school and receives counseling regarding the incidents, while the parents continue to seek compensation. In most of these cases, the schools and districts paid settlements before the cases were decided by the courts. In *Doe* v. *Petaluma City School District* (1993), the district court was the first to hold that student to student sexual harassment is actionable under Title IX (see discussion of school responsibility earlier in chapter). Although specifications for determining responsibility and liability are still not entirely clear, it has been firmly established by the above cases and others presented in this chapter that peer harassment is actionable behavior for suing a school or district.

The OCR ruling in *Modesto City Schools* (1993) reaffirms a school's responsibility to follow Title IX requirements in addressing misbehavior that is also sexual harassment. In the case, parents complained that their daughters had been subjected to an incident of physical harassment by fellow students, including fondling, at their elementary school. The school addressed this as a discipline problem, and talked to the offending boys, but did not address the incident as sexual harassment. A more serious incident, again involving physical harassment, occurred 4 months later. This time the school suspended the boys and transferred all but one to other schools. Again, the school did not investigate the incident or inform parents of their Title IX rights. The OCR found that the district violated Title IX when it treated sexual harassment as routine misbehavior and failed to investigate or inform the parents of their Title IX rights.

While most relevant cases demonstrate the increasing responsibility of schools to prevent peer harassment, *Aurelia D.* v. *Monroe County Board of Education* (1994) and *Mennone* v. *Gordon* (1995) suggest that schools are not responsible for peer harassment in all circumstances. In *Aurelia D.* v. *Monroe* (1994), a fifth-grade girl brought suit under Section 1983 claiming that her public school was slow to curtail harassment by a boy that included repeatedly trying to touch her breasts, rubbing against her, and using vulgar language. A district judge ruled that a school district was not liable for a student's harassment by another student since the public school did not have a special custodial relationship with its students or special duty to protect them from each other. While this case is being appealed, it suggests that the courts are ambivalent about the "custodial relationship" between schools and their students (EGCSH, 1993; Stein, 1995).

In *Mennone* v. *Gordon* (1995), a teacher was given qualified immunity from a charge of failing to protect a student from student to student harassment. Although the court concluded, contrary to other court decisions, that actions may be brought against individuals under Title IX, provided that they exercise a sufficient degree of control, the court found that this teacher's alleged failure of protection did not violate a right, as it would if it had involved abuse or harassment by a teacher against a student.

Oona R.-S. v. *Santa Rosa City Schools* (1995) addresses school district liability for both student to student harassment and the harassment of a student by a student teacher. In this case a sixth-grade female student sued her school district and several employees for sexual harassment by a student teacher and for creating a hostile environment for female students by failing to prevent male students from harassing them. The student's parents had informed school officials of the offensive conduct, but the officials did not remedy the problem and instead allegedly retaliated against the student. The student teacher's behavior toward Oona, in fondling her buttocks, whispering a nickname he had given to her into her ear, and sitting close to her with his legs straddling her body, was found to be intentional sexual harassment. The court also found that school officials could be liable for encouraging peer harassment, tolerating it, or failing to deter or punish it. In addition, reasonable school officials should have known that failing to adequately supervise the student teacher and tolerating or condoning the sexual harassment by other students were violations.

Same-Sex Peer Harassment

Schools and courts have been slow to recognize sexual harassment among same-sex individuals, including peers. However, the OCR has indicated that same-sex sexual harassment is protected under Title IX and the courts are moving to clarify this issue.

The OCR ruling in *East Side Union High School District* (1993) indicates that same-sex sexual harassment is protected under Title IX. In this instance, the school did not recognize same-sex sexual harassment while OCR did. The investigation concerned an incident in which a female student was the subject of a 6-month pattern of verbal and written sexual harassment (graffiti, taunts, rumors) by three female peers. The school did not see this as sexual harassment due to the fact that both victim and harassers were female, and thus did not investigate. The OCR found that the district violated Title IX when it failed to promptly and effectively stop the harassment, and that the district's grievance procedure failed to meet the "prompt and equitable standard of Title IX" (EGCSH, 1993, Appendix C, p. 309).

Seamons v. *Snow* (1994) is an important case since it was one of the first to deal with same-sex sexual harassment. A male high school student brought suit under Title IX claiming that he was forcibly stripped and taped to a towel rack in the school's locker room by his football teammates. Further, other students were encouraged to view him, including a female student whom the boy had taken to a school dance, who was shoved into the locker room. The student and his parents alleged that this hazing was well known to the coach and school officials, and that their complaints repeatedly were ignored or dismissed with responses such as "boys will be boys." The school did, however, cancel the rest of the football season, which served to increase harassment of the boy. A Federal District Court held that this was not an actionable case of hostile environment sexual harassment since the student failed to allege any concerted effort to discriminate on the basis of sex. The case is under appeal and will be considered along with other same-sex sexual harassment cases coming before the courts.

OFF-CAMPUS PROGRAMS AND ACTIVITIES*

School responsibility for prohibiting sexual harassment extends to off-campus programs and activities. This responsibility includes such events as team visits, study abroad, activities at extension sites, and exchange programs. Those schools whose programs of study require community service and clinical and applied experience may have particular interest in issues pertaining to off-campus placements. Such placements are an essential feature of school curricula for the preparation of professionals, including teachers, counselors, administrators, and health professionals.

Given the growing emphasis on school-to-work systems of education, it is likely that in the future more students from junior high through postsecondary levels will experience part of their learning in off-campus, work-based settings. Frequently a mentorship arrangement, requiring each student to work closely with a single individual, is part of the program design. The novelty and structure of such programs may create potential opportunities for sexual harassment. It will be important for schools to include policies, procedures, and educational strategies to avoid sexual harassment in school-to-work programs (see Chapters 4, 5, and 6).

The following example outlines issues of responsibility for a school of education whose students are placed for student teaching in K–12 school field placements and is illustrative for other off-campus situations. The discussion is based on a legal reading of rulings by the courts and the OCR and EEOC. The discussion will be helpful in suggesting general dimensions of responsibility and policy. However, the reader is advised that the conclusions are subject to interpretation, new court rulings, and the individual circumstances of each specific complaint. There is no single answer to the question of which institution (school of education or field placement school) is responsible when the student teacher working in a field placement is involved in sexual harassment, either as harasser or harassed. Such factors as the degree of supervision from the K–12 school and the school of education, how the placement site is selected, whether compensation or tuition is involved, and whether the student teacher is the harasser or harassed may have an impact on the degree of responsibility of the K–12 school and the school of education. The simplest answer to the question of who "owns" the problem in these circumstances is that both institutions own it. The

---

*Portions of this information have been published in Brandenburg (1995)

reader is advised to seek legal counsel when addressing any specific complaint of sexual harassment.

The following is based on consultation with counsel and a reading of court cases and rulings by the OCR and EEOC on this issue.*

I. The school of education and the field placement (K–12) site probably share responsibility for investigating an allegation of sexual harassment involving a student teacher at a field placement. The school of education likely would be held responsible to the extent it can be shown to control the circumstances surrounding the harassment. To avoid potential liability, the school of education at least should independently investigate any incident of which it has notice, whether the student teacher is the harassed or the harasser. Where the student teacher is the harassed, the school of education should respond to the complaints by taking corrective action within its control. The school of education also should act promptly, since delay in response may lead to liability. Where the student teacher is the alleged harasser of a K–12 student, staff person, or employee, the school of education would have legal responsibility only if it directly supervised the student teacher's actions, but should investigate and attempt to take corrective action in any event out of an abundance of caution.

II. A school of education must take all reasonable steps to avoid a hostile environment at its site and in the K–12 school. To avoid responsibility for hostile environment harassment at either setting, a school of education should (i) establish and publish grievance procedures for receiving and resolving complaints, and (ii) promptly investigate incidents of reported sexual harassment and, as supported by findings from the investigation, take appropriate corrective action. Once personnel in the school of education learn of a complaint, prompt action is essential, since delay may lead to liability. Although the school of education may have little control over a hostile environment at the K–12 school, the school of education nevertheless should establish and publish procedures, investigate, and, to the extent possible, attempt to resolve complaints.

To address sexual harassment at an off-campus field placement, a school should

1. Establish written policies and procedures on sexual harassment. Grievance procedures should include specific features to increase

---

*G. A. Davidson & C. A. Kerr, of Hughes, Hubbard & Reed, NY, personal communication, August 18, 1994.

their effectiveness, as described later. These policies and procedures should be discussed with the off-campus placement sites or K–12 settings. A school of education may wish to check the K–12 school's procedures to see if they conform to minimum standards of basic fairness. Consultation in advance might minimize later difficulty.

2. Orient students, faculty, supervisors, and field placement cooperating teachers about the issue of sexual harassment.
3. Urge students and advisors to report sexual harassment complaints and to use the formal grievance procedures.
4. Respond to complaints sympathetically and quickly, providing appropriate counseling services when necessary.
5. When accusations arise, at a minimum contact the K–12 school to see what can be done. Ensure that the avenues of communication between the institutions are understood prior to any complaints.
6. Conduct a thorough and objective investigation as quickly as possible.
7. Provide a "full remedy" for any harm that occurred and strive to prevent future occurrences.
8. Remove the student teacher from the hostile environment even as the investigation proceeds, if appropriate.

Although the school of education cannot control all aspects of a field placement, it needs to respond to sexual harassment complaints made, remove the student teacher (if possible), if the placement setting is hostile, and not place other students at that site if the situation there does not improve. The school of education may work collaboratively with K–12 field placement sites to encourage other institutions to become responsive to issues of sexual harassment. For example, joint discussions and orientation sessions might be held between personnel from the school of education and the K–12 setting, including cooperating teachers, supervisors, and student teachers. These sessions could include such issues as appropriate policies and practices, and how to handle complaints that arise. Schools that demonstrate best practice may be used as examples. There is no law suggesting that a school of education can be held liable for failing to inspect a field placement institution before permitting its students to be placed there. However, a school of education certainly should cease using a placement that has been problematic.

Whether the teacher candidate as observer, tutor, intern, or student teacher is the harassed, harasser, or third-party witness to sexual harassment at the K–12 field placement, the school of education should be informed and appropriate actions must begin as soon as possible. Arguably there are many circumstances in which the major responsibility for adjudicating an incident of sexual harassment rests with the field placement. Hopefully, the field placement will have sexual harassment policy and grievance procedures in place. However, given that many schools are not yet prepared with procedures, and that the school of education is responsible for prohibiting sexual harassment in its off-campus programs, it would be wise for the school of education to respond to complaints of sexual harassment reported by its students in field placements. The school of education should enlist the involvement of the K–12 school personnel and take action to investigate and resolve the matter.

Cases and Proceedings (Off Campus)

Moire v. *Temple University School of Medicine* (1986) involves an off-campus placement and was the first use of the EEOC Guidelines on Sexual Harassment and hostile environment sexual harassment under Title IX. The student claimed that while interning at an off-campus private psychiatric clinic, she was sexually harassed by the director of the clinic, and that faculty at her school conspired to protect him. The court ruled that the school "might be liable under Title IX to the extent it condoned or ratified any invidiously discriminatory conduct."

In *Lipsett* v. *University of Puerto Rico* (1988) the U.S. Court of Appeals for the First Circuit held that harassment by fellow students in a training program was actionable against a university under Title IX. In this case, a woman claimed that while she was in a residency training program, male residents sexually harassed her by decorating the communal restroom with sexual nicknames for all of the female residents, sexually explicit drawings of the student's body, and *Playboy* centerfolds. The court found that the university could be liable for hostile environment harassment if it had constructive knowledge of a hostile environment and failed to take steps to correct it. The director of the program had to have seen the offending materials since he used the same facility.

Murray v. *New York University College of Dentistry* (1995) suggests the limits to which a university can be held responsible under Title IX for sexual harassment in off-campus settings. In this case, the university was not held responsible for sexual harassment by a patient visiting a school clinic. A dental student alleged that a patient sexually harassed her from fall 1992 to summer 1993. During this time, she complained about the harassment to a faculty member on one occasion, who then talked to the patient. After failing six classes, the student was told she needed to repeat her second-year curriculum. She tried to make other arrangements to make up the classes, but claimed the harassment affected her performance. She also lodged a complaint at the college's EEO office, which took no action. In December 1993 she commenced the lawsuit, alleging Title IX discrimination by NYU for allowing the harassment to continue despite her having notified a professor, and for retaliating against her for asserting her Title IX rights. NYU successfully moved to dismiss the case. The court concluded that the plaintiff's allegations did not show that NYU had notice of ongoing sexual harassment sufficiently severe and pervasive to give rise to a hostile environment, or that after receiving notice NYU had taken any disadvantageous action that could have constituted retaliation. The court held that since the patient was not an agent of the college, the college was not liable for his conduct unless it had been notified that Murray was being subjected to a hostile environment and had failed to take action. This will be appealed.

Rosa H. v. *San Elizario Independent School District* (1995), which concerned school district liability for harassment by an after-school teacher, most of which took place off school property, listed six requirements that must be satisfied in order to successfully impute liability for a teacher's actions to a school district under Title IX: (1) the school district must be subject to Title IX (i.e., receive federal funds); (2) the person must have been subjected to intentional sexual harassment or abuse; (3) the harassment or abuse must have been by an employee of the school district; (4) the school district must have had notice, either actual or constructive, of the sexual harassment or abuse; (5) the school district must have failed to take prompt, effective, remedial measures; and (6) the conduct of the school district must have been negligent. Thus a student bringing a complaint must prove both intentional conduct by a school employee and negligent conduct by the school district.

These cases appear to have implications for other off-campus activities (including student teaching, counseling internships, etc.) and indicate that schools are responsible to their students both on and off campus. The particular circumstances will determine which institution has ultimate responsibility for incidents of sexual harassment that occur off campus. However, schools should have procedures for handling complaints by and against their students in other settings and should immediately investigate any complaint or suspicion of sexual harassment.

CONCLUSION

This chapter presents central federal statutes and regulations that prohibit sexual harassment in the workplace, K–12 schools, and institutions of higher education. Important legal cases and administrative proceedings on sexual harassment are reviewed to understand the legal responsibilities of educational institutions in the areas of extent of school responsibility, hostile environment, peer harassment, and off-campus programs. There are a number of clear implications that emerge from these laws, cases, and proceedings. All schools, from kindergarten to universities, as well as other places of work, should have written policies and procedures prohibiting sexual harassment. Lack of an adequate grievance procedure for sexual harassment complaints is in itself a violation of Title IX. The existence of such policies and procedures, however, is not in itself adequate. The institution must take timely action, follow its policies and procedures, and investigate whenever a complaint is received or harassment observed or suspected. Without procedures and strict adherence to them, an institution may be alleged to have a hostile environment and to tacitly encourage sexual harassment (see Chapter 4 and Appendix A).

Institutions must act to prevent both quid pro quo and hostile environment sexual harassment. They are responsible for the actions of employees, especially officers and supervisors. Schools may be responsible for student to student or peer harassment, including sexual harassment by same-sex individuals. Schools are also responsible for prohibiting sexual harassment in off-campus programs and activities. The example of a school of education placing a student teacher in a K–12 field placement is provided to illustrate the school's responsibility for preventing sexual harassment in off-campus programs. Schools should respond to a complaint of sexual harassment in an off-campus setting, move students from the setting if the environment is hostile, and develop programs to prepare students and faculty to identify and respond to sexual harassment in all settings.

ACKNOWLEDGMENTS

A special acknowledgment to Mr. Drew LaStella for his contributions to identifying and summarizing important legal cases and proceedings on sexual harassment and for his assistance in preparing this chapter. My appreciation to Mr. George Davidson and Ms. Carla A. Kerr of Hughes, Hubbard, and Reed, New York, for discussing and reporting on the legal responsibility schools have regarding the issue of sexual harassment in off-campus programs and activities. My thanks also for their review of the many cases and proceedings that we amassed, and for suggesting and summarizing some additional cases.

CHAPTER 3

Origins of Sexual Harassment

Sexual harassment is a manifestation of deeply held beliefs, attitudes, feelings, and cultural norms. In its most prevalent form, it is predicated on sociocultural views and sex-role stereotypes that males are active, dominant, and entitled to power, while females are passive, nurturing, submissive, and powerless. In sexual matters, when females say no, they mean yes. Ignorance and insensitivity between people contribute to sexual harassment. Changing sex roles and women's increased opportunities and assertiveness may intensify the anger, confusion, miscommunication, and misunderstanding that foster sexual harassment. Communication and understanding are flawed. Men who are threatened by the increasing competition from women in new roles and jobs may be angry and use power to sexually harass. Women empowered by change may now be more likely to object to unfair treatment and to declare and report sexual harassment.

"They just don't get it" is a refrain that is indeed accurate. Long-held stereotypes about gender retreat slowly. In addition, many, both males and females, still don't understand the issues and behaviors that constitute sexual harassment or for that matter why all the fuss. The subjective aspect of sexual harassment adds to the confusion when behavior that one person may encourage and consider fun may be experienced as harassment by someone else.

Voicing displeasure at certain behaviors is relatively recent. By the time something is said, the situation often has escalated so that explanations are not always clear or forthcoming. Pointing out sexual harassment during this critical period of societal and institutional change may contribute to the strain and is not without difficulty. However, eliminating sexual harassment holds the promise of improved relationships that are renegotiated and re-established in more constructive and respectful ways.

The firmly entrenched origins of sexual harassment make it difficult to eliminate. What schools can do to change these deeply held beliefs and attitudes must be based on an understanding of the complicated nature of sexual harassment and its underpinnings. This understanding is also necessary if we are to assist those caught in this behavior to better understand and to change their actions.

This chapter will discuss the origins and roots of sexual harassment; sex-role stereotypes; the impact of family, community, and schools; and the relationship of sexual harassment to other forms of discrimination. The discussion should suggest why it is difficult to deal with the problem of sexual harassment and at the same time suggest the bases for effective approaches to eliminating this behavior.

THEORIES

Sexual harassment is a complex behavior. Most theories and models describe sexual harassment as a way to obtain sex and/or to abuse or increase power (Stringer, Remick, Salisbury, & Ginorio, 1990). Tangri, Burt, and Johnson (1982) describe three models of sexual harassment based on an extensive review of the literature: (1) the Natural/Biological Model, which holds "that sexual harassment is simply natural sexual attraction between people" and posits that men have stronger sex drives that naturally predispose them "to aggress sexually against women, but without discriminatory intent" (p. 35); (2) the Organizational Model, which locates the cause of sexual harassment in institutional power structures; and (3) the Sociocultural Model, which "argues that sexual harassment reflects the larger society's differential distribution of power and status between the sexes" (p. 34). Sexual harassment is seen as a manifestation of the patriarchal system that socializes us to male aggressive/female passive norms. The research shows no clear support for any one model and suggests that sexual harassment is a complicated and not a single phenomenon (Gutek & Morasch, 1982; Tangri et al., 1982). Although not specified by the authors, each of these models seems to have a power component.

Some investigators see all instances of sexual harassment as an exploitation of a power relationship (Benson & Thomson, 1982; Carr, 1991; Fitzgerald et al., 1988; Paludi, 1990; Zalk, 1990), while others suggest that power is an insufficient explanation (Cleveland & Kerst, 1993; Gutek & Morasch, 1982; Pryor, La Vite, & Stoller, 1993). Those stressing power suggest that in our society, even when there is no apparent power component to an instance of sexual harassment, there is always a power differential between women and men.

While sexual harassment often involves an abuse of power and a gender power differential does exist, power exploitation does not explain all instances of sexual harassment. Sexual harassment by subordinates (contrapower harassment) (Benson, 1984), between persons of similar role status, and among persons of the same sex, are unexplained by this theory. For purposes of this book, we will consider sexual harassment as a behavior that differentially involves both sex and power.

A promising area of research to explain sexual harassment examines culturally determined attitudes and beliefs and suggests a relationship between traditional sex-role stereotypes and sexual harassment. A connection has been demonstrated between attitudes toward sexual harassment and attitudes regarding gender and sex roles (Gutek & Morasch, 1982; Murrell & Dietz-Uhler, 1993; Pryor, 1987; Vaux, 1993). Attitudes toward sexual harassment are strongly related to beliefs about men and women and their social interaction. Adversarial sexual beliefs (defined as the belief that sexual relationships are fundamentally exploitive) predict attitudes toward sexual harassment for men and women (Murrell & Dietz-Uhler, 1993). The likelihood of sexual harassment is positively related to adversarial sexual beliefs, rape myth acceptance, and sex-role stereotyping (i.e., beliefs that blame the victim and see women as liking rape), and negatively related to the capacity to take on someone else's perspective (Pryor, 1987). These connections suggest the way not only to understand sexual harassment but also to develop educational interventions to foster change.

The connections between sex-role stereotyping and sexual harassment can be inferred from a review of the literature on rape. Rape seems to fall on a continuum of sexual aggression, as an extension of traditional stereotypic beliefs and attitudes about gender (Bell et al., 1992; Briere & Malamuth, 1983; Check & Malamuth, 1983). Sex-role stereotyping and adversarial sexual beliefs are strongly related to rape myth acceptance and the self-reported likelihood of rape (Briere & Malamuth, 1983; Burt, 1980; Check & Malamuth, 1983; Sandberg, Jackson, & Petretic-Jackson, 1987). Attitudes about women, rape, and rapists serve to release or excuse sexual aggression (Bell et al., 1992; Burt, 1980). Aggression against women seems to be a reflection of cultural attitudes and norms that assign male active/female passive roles, and foster beliefs such as women mean yes when they say no and enjoy aggressive and even coerced sex.

Burt (1980) found that rape myth acceptance varies directly with sex-role stereotyping and adversarial sexual beliefs (i.e., beliefs that force and coercion are legitimate ways to gain compliance with intimate and sexual relationships). Antecedents to rape seem to be cultural, socially transmitted attitudes about women, rape, and rapists. These attitudes are posited as releasers of sexual aggression.

In an interesting study, both women and men showed a similar connection between their sex-role stereotyping and reactions to rape or rape myth acceptance, and were less likely to label acquaintance rape as rape (Check & Malamuth, 1983). Subjects with high scores on sex-role stereotyping thought that women reacted favorably to rape (i.e., enjoyed it), and stated that they were more likely to rape. High-stereotyping individuals showed identical arousal patterns to those of rapists. Those who reported that they were most likely to rape did not see the negative effects of rape.

The extent to which some women and men subscribe to gender stereotypes and rape myths contributes to the difficulty and misunderstandings that occur in intimate social situations. Is it any wonder that miscommunication and confusion result? It is critical to educate and to help people unravel the attitudes and behaviors involved.

IMPACT OF FAMILY AND COMMUNITY

The roots of sexual harassment are seen in the attitudes, values, and perceptions that surround and shape the socialization of children and the development of gender identity. At the most basic level are the meanings that we attach to gender: what we expect from a girl instead of a boy.

Gender identity can be traced back to birth and early childhood. Americans stereotype children by the birth congratulations cards we send (Bridges, 1993). Cards for boy babies are usually blue and emphasize physical activity, whereas those for girls are pink and contain fewer messages of joy and happiness than those for boys (Pomerleau, Bolduc, Malcuit, & Cossette, 1990). Parents are still raising girls and boys very differently, and they are still encouraging "sex-typed play by selecting different toys for female and male children, even before the child can express her or his own preferences" (Pomerleau et al., 1990, p. 365). By their twenty-fifth month, boys play with significantly more sports equipment, tools, and vehicles; girls are given significantly more kitchen appliances and utensils. Play and the related experiences promote skills development and the adoption of roles that enhance abilities related to particular occupations. For example, the active exploration necessary in the physical sciences is far more encouraged in boys than in girls (Vandell, 1989).

Throughout childhood, sex-role stereotypes are reinforced by the media and society. Television, sports heroes, military leaders, and books tell us that males should be active, independent, and aggressive

(Scott, 1982). A female stereotype that is passive, inactive, and dependent is visible in children's literature and on television (Davis, 1990; Purcell & Stewart, 1990). In spite of some increased sensitivity in the media over the last decade, girls and women still appear less frequently than men, and they are shown largely in sex-stereotyped roles. By age 6 or 7, "children have clear ideas about gender" and "both boys and girls strive for conformity with gender stereotyped roles" (AAUW, 1992, p. 10).

Boys and girls get different messages regarding sexual responsibility. In nursery school, parents tend to watch and warn their daughters regarding sexual and aggressive activity, while they talk less with their sons about these issues. It is a girl's job to protect herself, while boys, who are physically and sexually aggressive, "are doing what comes naturally" and their behavior may be excused (Sapon-Shevin & Goodman, 1992). A dramatic example and possible consequence of encouraging aggressiveness in males is the "Spur Posse." This group of teenage boys pursued and kept score of the number of young females they sexually abused. When interviewed about the group, the father of one of the boys proudly boasted: "Aren't they virile specimens?" (Gross, 1993a, p. A13).

IMPACT OF SCHOOLS

Gender stereotypes that permeate our culture and set the context for sexual harassment unfortunately are reinforced in our schools. Myra and David Sadker, in their excellent book, *Failing at Fairness* (1994), document the ways schools from the earliest grades reinforce sex-role stereotypes and are unfair to girls. "As teachers use their expertise to question, praise, prove, clarify and correct boys, they help these male students sharpen ideas, refine their thinking, gain their voice and achieve more. When female students are offered the leftovers of teacher time and attention, morsels of amorphous feedback, they achieve less" (Sadker & Sadker, 1994, p. 13). Teachers initiate more communications with boys, call on boys more frequently, and give boys more attention than girls when they misbehave. Teachers spend more time with girls in reading classes and more time with boys in math. As teachers comment, they are more likely to attribute a boy's shortcomings to a lack of effort and a girl's to a lack of ability (AAUW, 1992; Vandell, 1989). Teachers solve problems raised by girls, and explain how to solve those raised by boys (Hall & Sandler, 1982). They ask boys more complex, abstract, and open-ended questions, and they are more likely to praise a boy's work for intellectual content (Sadker & Sadker, 1982).

A similar picture emerges in the American Association of University Women 1992 study of kindergarten through twelfth-grade schools. The study reports that boys are valued more than girls, teachers give more attention to boys, and sexual harassment is tolerated or ignored. "Whether one looks at pre-schools, classrooms or university lecture halls, at female teachers or male teachers, research spanning the last twenty years consistently reveals that males receive more teacher attention than do females" (AAUW, 1992, p. 68).

It is not simply teachers' attitudes and pedagogy that contribute to reinforcing these behaviors, but curricular materials, including textbooks, literature, media, and so on. Later chapters will suggest resources and strategies to develop bias-free curricula (see Chapters 5, 6, and Appendix B).

The differential treatment of boys and girls in the classroom fosters lower self-esteem among girls and reinforces the biases that lie beneath and result in sexual harassment. The perception that boys are more valued than girls, who are second-class citizens, fosters the notion that it is acceptable to treat girls poorly. If, through giving boys most of our attention and forgiving their inappropriate behavior, we give them the message that they are more worthy and powerful than girls, is it any surprise that boys attempt to use this power? "The ways students treat each other during school hours is an aspect of the informal learning process, with significant negative implications for girls. There is mounting evidence that boys do not treat girls well" (AAUW, 1992, p. 73).

Unfortunately, school authorities may not take the issue of sexual harassment seriously. They may not yet understand the continuum that exists from undervaluing girls and encouraging aggressive behavior in boys, to tolerating pranks and "innocent teasing" of girls, to accepting sexist content in texts, to "playing rape" in the school yard, and finally to sexual harassment, including dramatic instances of sexual abuse. "When blatantly sexual or sexist remarks become an accepted part of classroom conversations, female students are degraded. Sexual harassment in business and the military now causes shock waves and legal suits. Sexual harassment in schools is dismissed as normal and unavoidable 'boys will be boys' behavior, but by being targeted girls are being intimidated and caused to feel like members of an inferior class" (Sadker & Sadker, 1994, p. 13). Such actions as boys rating girls on attractiveness and teasing girls to make them cry are examples of "boys being boys" behavior. These actions that appear to go unnoticed and unreported have terrible consequences. The message is that it is okay to harass. We need to examine why these attitudes prevail, and what it would take to make school personnel more aware of the implications and seriousness of so-called innocent interactions.

RACE AND ETHNICITY

A confluence of issues is suggested regarding sexual harassment and other characteristics such as race, class, and sexual orientation, which leave people open to discrimination and diminish their power in our society. Since sexual harassment is an issue involving power, it shares many characteristics of other forms of discrimination. The concepts of "gender power" and "ethnic power" refer to the culture attributing more power to men than to women, and more power to whites than to people of color (Stringer et al., 1990). Given this power component of sexual harassment, it would not be surprising if groups traditionally excluded from social power structures were especially victimized by sexual harassment. While there is some support for this observation, there has been no systematic study of the factors involved.

In the 1970s, when incidents of sexual harassment on campus were first made public, the anecdotal reports involved an overrepresentation of people of color as both harassed and harasser. Gradually, this observation has been supported by quantitative data. "Many of the earlier quid pro quo and condition of work cases were brought forth by minority women who were being singled out as targets for both sexual and racial harassment" (Strock-Lynskey & Fuchs, 1987, p. 3).

African-Americans are more likely to have been victims of many forms of sexual harassment, especially forms involving contact (AAUW, 1993). For example, 49% of African-American girls, as compared with 37% white girls, reported having their clothes pulled, 48% of African-American and 36% of white girls reported being cornered, and 30% of African-American and 22% of white girls reported being forced to kiss. "Among African-Americans, the incidence of harassment involving direct physical contact is alarming" (AAUW, 1993, p. 25).

After graduating, women of color experience high levels of sexual harassment in the workplace, and file a disproportionate number of sexual harassment complaints. In fact, the first Supreme Court case on sexual harassment was brought by a black woman (*Meritor Savings Bank* v. *Vinson*, 1986). A study that surveyed 29,771 university and college faculty found only a slightly higher rate of sexual harassment for African-Americans as compared with women of different racial/ethnic groups. After adjusting for length of service, women faculty reported that they had been sexually harassed at their current institution as follows: African-Americans, 16.2%; whites, 15.4%; Native-Americans, 14.6%; Latinos, 14%; and Asian-Americans, 13.7% (Dey, Sax, & Korn, 1994).

People of color often have been excluded from positions of power, the subject of ongoing discrimination, and financially vulnerable. In college, they frequently must rely on financial aid and loans. In the job market they make 51.3% of the average salaries for white males, and are most visible in low-paying, low-status jobs (DeFour, 1990). Given their tenuous financial position, women of color are more vulnerable to their harassers—to resist or speak up could very well put them out of a job and adversely affect their families.

Stereotypes about women of color also contribute to increasing their chances of being harassed. "These images either portray the woman as weak and thus unlikely to fight back if harassed, or they are perceived as very sexual and thus desiring sexual attention" (DeFour, 1990, p. 48). The problems of women of color are further exacerbated when they consider the possibility of bringing a sexual harassment complaint as having to make a choice between their gender and their race. Social pressures may prohibit airing problems outside of the community. When the harasser belongs to one's race or group, there are strong disincentives to making the problem public and causing trouble for a colleague. The analogous dynamic has been observed on the college campus when a student bringing sexual harassment charges against a male student athlete loses the support of her friends for "betraying" a fellow student. These issues have an impact on the reporting of sexual harassment and may result in even greater underreporting of sexual harassment by people of color. Grievance procedures that do not guarantee confidentiality to the person reporting an instance of sexual harassment (as discussed in Chapter 4) may lower the reporting even further.

SEXUAL ORIENTATION

There are many complicating issues involved in the sexual harassment of homosexual persons. To the concepts of gender power and ethnic power, I propose adding "sexual orientation power" to reflect the cultural attribution of more power to heterosexuals than to homosexuals. This power inequality may be reinforced by the denigration of "female or feminine" traits and behaviors, which is especially severe when the feminine traits are found in males. It is often difficult to distinguish between discrimination based on sexual orientation and sexual harassment "since the two are intertwined and tend to be manifested in the same ways" (NYSGTF, 1993, p. 73).

The harassment of gay men and lesbians has its own set of issues. In addition to sexual harassment, gay and lesbian persons may experience harassment due to sexual orientation. If an employee who is homosexual complains about being sexually harassed, he or she may face additional penalties and discrimination for revealing sexual orientation, such as being "outed" by co-workers and being subjected to derogatory insults. These problems are exacerbated by a general lack of societal support for gays. The pressure to remain hidden keeps many gays and lesbians more alone than other minority groups. These dynamics require schools to be particularly sensitive in creating a climate, policies, and procedures that serve all members of the community.

CONCLUSION

Sexual harassment is a complicated behavior that is not exclusively a sexual issue. Frequently, but not always, sexual harassment is related to issues of power and sex involving the exploitation of a power relationship. This book considers sexual harassment as socioculturally determined behavior that differentially involves both sex and power.

Sexual harassment is closely linked to and may have its genesis in sex-role attitudes and stereotypes. The roots of sexual harassment are located in the socialization of children and the development of gender identity. Unfortunately, family, school, and society all socialize children in ways that tend to devalue girls and foster sexual harassment. School personnel too often assume the attitude that "boys will be boys" and do not take sexual harassment seriously. They fail to see the continuum that exists from undervaluing girls and encouraging aggressive behavior in boys, to tolerating pranks and "innocent teasing" of girls, to accepting sexist content in texts, to "playing rape" in the school yard, and finally to sexual harassment including instances of sexual abuse.

The past 2 decades have seen dramatic changes in sex roles (particularly the role of women) and increased cultural diversity. While great progress has been made in moving away from sex-role stereotypes and achieving equity and opportunities for all groups, it is not without some negative consequences.

"This is better than winning Miss America for me," proclaimed Flora Tartakovsky, one of four female top-ten winners of the prestigious 1994 Westinghouse Science Talent Search ("Three New York Students," 1994, p. B3). The success of young women in the Westinghouse Science Talent Search echoes the dramatic progress in the representation of women in traditionally male majors and careers. For example, in just 20 years between 1974 and 1994, women degree recipients have gone from 15% to 43% in law degrees; 13% to 36% in medicine; 15% to 44% in management; and 6% to 70% in veterinary medicine (National Center for Educational Statistics, 1994). Progress is slower in certain areas, such as engineering, chemistry, and physics.

On the negative side, the rapid changes sometimes have strained relationships, compounded communication issues, and made it more likely that people will experience (and fortunately protest) sexual harassment. Upon entering many professions, women still face the so-called "glass ceiling," which caps their level of attainment. Women continue to suffer the negative attitudes and behaviors, including sexual harassment, that remain in the educational and work settings.

The increasing diversity of our schools and colleges, which continue to welcome and encourage people from very different backgrounds, creates new dimensions of complexity. Unfortunately, along with the richness of diversity come the differences in cultural norms, language, and worldviews that make misperception and miscommunication more likely. Those groups without power, including women, people of color, religious minorities, and gays and lesbians, may be more likely to experience sexual harassment. Our educational institutions must not only encourage increased diversity and opportunity, but do more to ensure understanding and a sense of community in schools that are free of sexual harassment. An understanding of the origins of sexual harassment suggests the complexity and tenacity of this behavior and should assist schools in developing strategies to prevent its occurrence.

CHAPTER 4

Creating Policies and Grievance Procedures

The deeply entrenched origins of sexual harassment described in the preceding chapter suggest why this behavior is difficult to change. Addressing sexual harassment requires a multidimensional approach that includes the short-term strategy of creating strong sexual harassment policies and grievance procedures and the long-term strategy of employing education (described in Chapters 5 and 6). A school that develops strong sexual harassment policies and grievance procedures takes what may be the most important short-term steps to address and prevent sexual harassment. Educational institutions reveal their priorities and values through their policies and procedures. An institution with strong sexual harassment policies and grievance procedures emphasizes the importance it places on this issue and on equal opportunity. Studies suggest that the rate of sexual harassment complaints is related to the perception of sex equity at the institution and that institutions with strong policies and procedures have fewer sexual harassment complaints (Hoffman, 1986; LaFontaine & Tredeu, 1986; Shakeshaft & Cohan, 1995). Sexual harassment policies and grievance procedures contribute to a sense of equity, reduce sexual harassment, and meet legal requirements.

All schools, from prekindergarten to universities, should have policies prohibiting sexual harassment. Educational institutions that receive federal funds are legally required to prevent sex discrimination and sexual harassment, ensure a nonhostile environment, and provide a grievance procedure to deal with sexual harassment complaints. Title IX requires these institutions to "adopt and publish a grievance procedure providing for prompt and equitable resolution of student and employee complaints" (OCR, 1987, p. 2). As employers, they must also follow the EEOC guidelines to enforce Title VII. Without written procedures and strict adherence to them, an institution may be alleged to have a hostile environment and to tacitly encourage sexual harassment. Thus, establishing strong sexual harassment policies and grievance procedures is a crucial step in addressing sexual harassment, even as it is required by law and necessary to protect the institution from litigation.

This chapter presents a rationale for sexual harassment policies and grievance procedures. The chapter describes essential components of a model grievance procedure, difficult dilemmas, the issue of false accusations, and special institutional responsibilities for responding to sexual harassment in off-campus programs and activities. Examples of state, local, and school sexual harassment policies and grievance procedures are provided in Appendix A.

Currently, a majority of postsecondary institutions, but few primary and secondary schools, have established sexual harassment policies and procedures. A report from the New York State Governor's Task Force on Sexual Harassment (NYSGTF) (1993) suggests that only a limited number of K–12 school systems have sexual harassment policies and grievance procedures in place. "The Task Force's finding from its focus groups that few schools have such procedures suggests that compliance with Title IX by schools in New York State is less than satisfactory" (NYSGTF, 1993, p. 113). A study of sexual abuse by Shakeshaft and Cohan (1995) including 225 school districts (184 in New York State and 41 in other states) found that most districts did not have procedures to report sexual abuse or to respond to such complaints. The authors noted that many districts developed policies and procedures only after a lawsuit. The study concluded that those districts that had fewer incidents of sexual abuse had the following in common: (1) strong and clear policies concerning sexual harassment, (2) employees and students who know the policies and how to file complaints, and (3) students and staff who are educated about sexual harassment and what to do if sexual harassment occurs (Shakeshaft & Cohan, 1995, p. 519).

A limited number of states have enacted laws that require schools to have policies and procedures on sexual harassment. California requires policies and procedures from prekindergarten through postgraduate school. Minnesota and Massachusetts "have implemented significant sexual harassment prevention strategies in elementary and secondary schools" (NYSGTF, 1993, p. 97). Washington State, South Dakota, and Tennessee have such requirements only at the postsecondary level. "In New York and most other states, the problem of sexual harassment in schools, particularly at the elementary and secondary levels, has only been acknowledged recently" (NYSGTF, 1993, p. 97).

A survey of colleges and universities (Robertson, Dyer, & Campbell, 1988) showed that in 1988 only 66% of postsecondary institutions had sexual harassment policy statements and only 46% had written procedures. At that time, most of the policies included a definition of sexual harassment that emphasized sexual activity through coercion or force, rather than a hostile working or academic environment. A more recent study suggests that a greater number of universities and colleges have written procedures and that policies more often include hostile environment sexual harassment (Brandenburg, 1994a). Recent case law that clarifies the meaning of "hostile environment" as well as the liability of educational institutions has stimulated more institutions to develop sexual harassment policies and procedures.

Some critics suggest that the notion of "hostile environment" is too vague and object to schools taking any responsibility in this area. The critics argue that adoption of such a broad definition of sexual harassment by the institution violates academic freedom. They therefore demand that the definition of sexual harassment in school policies be confined to individual behavior that is manifestly sexual and that clearly violates the rights of others (National Association of Scholars, 1994).

Sexual harassment policies can and should be reconciled with the rights and freedoms of the individual. It is important for school policies and procedures to clarify the definition of sexual harassment and to provide specific examples of behaviors in the context of the rights of the individual. With appropriate care and sensitivity, it is possible to develop clear policies that do not infringe on individual rights. In addition, even as these issues are being clarified, schools are legally required to include both quid pro quo and hostile environment harassment in their policies and procedures (see cases in Chapter 2).

POLICIES

Sexual harassment policies are most effective when they provide definitions sufficiently broad to capture the scope of the problem, but specific enough to describe behavioral examples. A policy should indicate the audience being addressed: school employees, students, faculty, or all of the academic community. Schools are realizing the need to include peer harassment as part of the policy statement. Sexual harassment policies should clearly state that student to student sexual harassment is prohibited and subject to disciplinary measures.

A sexual harassment policy may be part of a general discrimination policy prohibiting several forms of harassment or a separate policy focusing specifically on sexual harassment. The general harassment policy may include sexual harassment along with harassment of all legally protected groups and indicate that all persons are protected from mistreatment. A general policy that includes sexual harassment should clearly define this behavior and state who is covered by the policy. A separate sexual harassment policy should highlight the seriousness of this offense and describe how it differs from other forms of harassment. Primary and secondary schools typically have adopted a single general discrimination policy. Postsecondary institutions most often have developed separate sexual harassment policies and sometimes separate procedures for sexual harassment complaints.

Consensual Relationships

As a supplement to sexual harassment policies, some schools include a statement about consensual relationships between students and staff. For example, the University of Iowa's campus-wide policy on sexual harassment declares that the inherent power imbalance between the supervisor or teacher and the student prohibits faculty members from having amorous relationships with students in their classes or under their supervision. The policy also advises against consensual relationships with students outside of the instructional context since "relationships that the parties view as consensual may appear to others to be exploitive" (University of Iowa, 1986). The State University of New York at Albany describes consensual student–instructor relationships as unethical when the instructor has professional responsibility over the student, and warns against such relationships outside of the instructional context (State University of New York at Albany, 1991). Some K–12 schools also address this problem. For example, the Hotchkiss School explicitly prohibits employees from making any sexual advances toward students in light of the school's role *in loco parentis* (Hotchkiss School, 1993—see Appendix A).

GRIEVANCE PROCEDURES

Schools that receive federal funding are required to have a clear complaint procedure that encourages the reporting of incidents of sexual harassment. As with policies, grievance procedures may be general for all types of harassment or separate for sexual harassment complaints. A general procedure may have an advantage for those instances of harassment that involve multiple issues, such as a complaint that involves issues of race and age along with sexual harassment. A general procedure also may reduce the number of separate procedures needed by an institution. A separate procedure has the advantage of focusing more attention on the unique aspects of the problem of sexual harassment. It emphasizes the seriousness of the problem and allows those implementing the procedure to focus their understanding and training.

Grievance procedures available within a school (internal) are more likely than procedures available through outside agencies (OCR and the courts) to be responsive to sexual harassment complaints by members of the school community. Internal grievance procedures may save time, minimize emotional and financial expense, and be more sensitive to all persons. Moreover, persons may first seek redress through internal procedures and continue to have recourse to outside avenues of complaint. The responsiveness of an institution's procedures will determine whether members of the community turn to an internal system or to an outside process (Brandenburg, 1982). It is important for all members of the academic community to be involved in the process of developing sexual harassment grievance procedures. Input from all constituencies will increase the likelihood of developing grievance procedures that are viewed as comprehensive and effective.

Models

Schools have developed several models of sexual harassment grievance procedures. The two most typical models include: (1) designating a single person as grievance officer, and (2) establishing a grievance board or committee.

Grievance Officer Model

The grievance officer model is most common in postsecondary institutions. For example, of 11 universities in New York State, eight had grievance officers and two had a grievance board (Brandenburg, 1994a). In the officer model, sexual harassment complaints are brought to the attention of one designated individual, often an affirmative action officer, human resource person, ombuds person, or student affairs staff member. The officer usually receives some training and provides consultation and support through informal and formal procedures. Schools typically indicate a channel through which the officer can be contacted. Often, the officer hears complaints and concerns about all forms of harassment and discrimination in the institution.

The grievance officer model has both advantages and disadvantages. Advantages include clarity as to who receives complaints and a reduction of administrative layers. The major disadvantage is that there is only one point of entry into the complaint process. This becomes problematic when the harassed person does not feel comfortable discussing his or her concerns with the designated grievance officer. An additional disadvantage is the frequent perception that the delegated person is part of the administrative structure and is unlikely to be fair. Unfortunately, institutions that do not clarify the process that will be followed during a complaint contribute to this lack of trust.

Grievance Board Model

The second most common model for receiving complaints of sexual harassment in academic institutions is a grievance board or committee. A board or committee is appointed to accept complaints, mediate between parties, and recommend sanctions (Brandenburg, 1982). Grievance boards may comprise equal numbers of women and men who represent different disciplines and constituencies within the institution, including students. The board typically is selected by the dean or principal based on recommendations of others in the academic community.

The grievance board has a number of advantages over the grievance officer model. Notably, the grievance board offers multiple avenues of access to the process and increases the likelihood that a person will find someone with whom they are comfortable to discuss a complaint. In addition, the grievance board structure allows a wider number of school constituencies to feel represented in the process. This model may be established outside the usual channels of institutional authority and therefore be perceived as more independent, representative, and fair. Disadvantages of this model as compared with a single officer model are that it requires greater communication and coordination as well as increased measures to ensure confidentiality.

One variation on the grievance board model that is used by some institutions involves the selection and training of a large pool of individuals from the academic community to hear many types of harassment complaints. When an incident of harassment arises, a subcommittee is selected from the pool of trained teachers, administrators, employees, and students to best fit the specific needs of the complaint. For example, if the complaint involves an incident of sexual harassment between persons from two different academic units, the subcommittee will be selected to include representatives of the two areas involved.

Stages of the Grievance Procedure

It is important for the community to be acquainted with the steps of the grievance process, irrespective of the model used. This knowledge tends to make the procedure less mysterious and more approachable. The process often includes informal and formal stages. Cases involving serious offenses and the likelihood of serious sanctions (e.g., loss of job or expulsion) may involve additional disciplinary procedures.

Informal Stage

The informal stage is the most important part of the grievance procedure. During this stage a person may seek advice or assistance in resolving a matter without submitting a signed complaint. Most procedures include an informal stage that handles the majority of reported instances of sexual harassment (Robertson et al., 1988; Rowe, 1996). People are more inclined to seek assistance and to resolve the problem informally than to file a formal grievance that involves an adversarial process. Most people who have been sexually harassed want to end the behavior, not punish the harasser (Riger, 1991; Robertson et al., 1988; Rowe, 1996). New York State universities reported an average of 10 informal and five formal sexual harassment complaints a year (Brandenburg, 1994b).

Informal procedures can be flexible and responsive. During the informal stage a complaint officer or board member can mediate among the parties and sometimes assist the person bringing a complaint in speaking directly to the person complained against. Often, complaints of sexual harassment may be resolved through mediation, conciliation, and problem solving, during the informal stage of a grievance procedure. However, this is not always possible, and persons with complaints also should be advised that they may file a formal complaint, take the complaint directly to the Office for Civil Rights, and bring a private lawsuit (Brandenburg, 1982).

Formal Stage

The formal stage of a grievance procedure requires a signed written complaint. The goal of this stage of the process is to determine the guilt or innocence of the person complained against. The process usually involves an investigation, hearing, adjudication, and possible appeal. This stage has been described as rights-based and adversarial (Rowe,

1996). Once the complaint is filed, control rests with the grievance board or grievance officer. Sometimes, particularly when serious sanctions are recommended, the formal stage of the grievance procedure may trigger another disciplinary process for the person accused (student, faculty, or staff) (see AAUP, 1995; Yale College, 1979–1995a).

Components of an Effective Grievance Procedure

The following components of a grievance procedure may increase its effectiveness, irrespective of the model:

1. The policy statement prohibiting sexual harassment and describing grievance procedures should include clear definitions of the behaviors covered.
2. The statement should be widely publicized.
3. A person on campus should be designated as the Title IX compliance officer and his or her name and address made available to the community.
4. A sexual harassment advisor or counselor should be appointed.
5. More than one person should be designated as the point of entry into the process (a specific group of people should be designated by name).
6. A grievance board or panel that represents campus or school constituents should be designated to receive sexual harassment complaints.
7. Persons responsible for handling complaints should be trained.
8. The investigative, advocacy, and judgment roles of the grievance procedure should be clearly distinguished.
9. Symmetry in protecting the rights of the person complaining and the person accused should be provided.
10. The procedure should include an informal as well as a formal stage.
11. Confidentiality should be an integral part of the procedure and ensured to the extent possible.
12. Prompt and timely adjudication should be the goal of the process.
13. A thorough and impartial investigation of complaints, including an opportunity for the complainants to present evidence, should be included.
14. The procedures should note that interim corrective action during an investigation may be appropriate (e.g., change of off-campus placement).
15. Designated time frames for the filing, investigation, and resolution of complaints should be included.

16. Results should be communicated to involved parties at the end of the investigation.
17. The right to appeal an outcome should be included.
18. False accusations as well as retaliation against those making honest complaints should be prohibited.
19. An annual summary of complaints should be published that provides the gender and status of the persons involved. For example:

Complainant	Respondent	Resolution
Female undergraduate student	Female teaching assistant	Warning

20. The campus as well as off-campus placement sites should be educated about the issue of sexual harassment.

It is difficult to determine the effectiveness of sexual harassment policies and procedures. Indicators of effectiveness include the extent to which the school community is aware of policies and procedures and the extent to which they are perceived as equitable. Further indications may be based on the number of incidents of sexual harassment that occur and the number of complaints brought to the grievance procedure. However, it is difficult to discern whether a low number of reported complaints is due to a low incidence of sexual harassment or the result of a lack of confidence in the grievance procedures. Riger (1991), in an excellent analysis of existing procedures, makes an interesting case for gender bias inherent in grievance procedures. She argues that current procedures are based on a power system that favors men and is biased against women. She suggests that women prefer the informal stage of a procedure where the complainant can retain more control of the process. Rowe (1996) analyzes grievance procedure designs and proposes the "Integrated Dispute Resolution System" as the most effective model (p. 14). This system includes informal and formal stages as described above. Many of its strongest features were anticipated by the Yale College *Grievance Procedure for Complaints of Sexual Harassment* included in Appendix A (Brandenburg, 1982; Rowe, 1996; Yale College, 1979–1995a).

Difficult Dilemmas

The descriptions above suggest the main features of contemporary sexual harassment grievance procedures. While these procedures seem to be effective in most cases, some dilemmas remain. Those being hotly debated on college campuses include: (1) the rights of the individual bringing a complaint versus the responsibility of the institution to provide a nonhostile environment; (2) confidentiality of records versus the need for information regarding repeat offenders; and (3) due process versus collegial mediation.

The Rights of the Individual Bringing a Complaint Versus the Responsibility of the School to Provide a Nonhostile Environment

How does an academic institution protect the confidentiality of a person who reports what might be an instance of sexual harassment and asks that no action be taken, while meeting its responsibility to prevent and respond to sexual harassment? The following is not an infrequent occurrence.

A student speaks to a member of the grievance board about an incident that, if true, constitutes a serious instance of sexual harassment. After sharing the incident the student indicates that she wants her confidentiality maintained and pleads that no action be taken. The board member is torn: She respects the student's desire for confidentiality, but she is also eager to prevent a hostile environment, protect others, and do something about the "harasser." Dilemma: Schools are legally required to prevent sexual harassment and a hostile environment. Thus institutions are obligated to respond when made aware of sexual harassment. However, if persons bringing a complaint cannot be ensured confidentiality and a degree of control, few people are likely to bring complaints forward.

Currently, a number of institutions are struggling with this issue. Cornell University, in revising its sexual harassment procedures, considered including the condition, "If the Office of Equal Opportunity determines that the allegations in a complaint are grave and may be well founded, then the Office of Equal Opportunity reserves the right to continue in its own name any investigation that the complaining party does not wish to pursue" (Annese, 1995, p. 10). At Stanford University sexual harassment procedures indicate that "confidentiality cannot be maintained . . . when the university is required by law to disclose information (such as in response to legal process) and when disclosure is required by the University's outweighing interest in protecting the rights of others" (Stanford University, 1995, p. 7). Alternatively, Yale College's grievance procedures state, "The board will respect the wishes of the student making the complaint regarding further investigation and will not carry a specific complaint forward without the student's explicit permission or instruction" (Yale College, 1979–1995a, p. 1).

While I appreciate the dilemma and the institution's concern that it will be held responsible if no action is taken to prevent sexual harassment, a breach of confidentiality seems counterproductive. I suspect that students will cease to bring sexual harassment complaints to a procedure that may not guarantee their confidentiality. Thus, if people experiencing sexual harassment do not come forward, the institution will be poorly informed and have an even greater vulnerability to accusations of hostile environment and inaction. In addition, the school's response is limited without the participation of the person being harassed and a signed formal complaint. It seems preferable for schools to take forceful and creative measures against sexual harassment, while respecting the confidentiality of community members. Such measures would include generic efforts directed at education about sexual harassment that reach the person named (e.g., a meeting to discuss sexual harassment with the athletic coaches, including the coach identified to the grievance officer). (See further discussion in the Conclusions.)

Confidentiality of Records Versus the Need for Information About Repeat Offenders

Often people being harassed seek to discuss their experiences but do not wish to file a formal complaint. In these circumstances and without any formal complaints, the grievance officer or board member may become aware of a number of alleged instances of sexual harassment without a reason to inform the persons accused. Since sexual harassment behavior often is repeated, a history of such conversations may reveal a pattern involving the same persons. For this reason it is useful to have a history of informal complaints. Unfortunately, there may be a negative side to retaining records in what sometimes has been dubbed the "locked box" approach. This occurs when accusations are retained without alerting the person accused and giving that person the opportunity to provide an alternative explanation. Dilemma: Retaining secret undocumented accusations is unfair. However, the lack of any records may protect "repeat offenders."

There are a number of ways to address this dilemma and to be fair to the person accused as well as to the person bringing a complaint. Some procedures retain records of formal complaints only, or of those complaints where the person accused has been informed. Some procedures hold records for a limited time or until there is a clear disposition of the matter. I have participated in a process that includes complaints of limited identification, in which the confidentiality of the person discussing a complaint is preserved while a discussion is held with the person accused. If handled sensitively and fairly, this conversation, although not particularly comfortable, eventually may be welcomed by the person accused. It serves to educate about sexual harassment and actually may spare the person accused from a more serious or formal complaint in the future (Yale College, 1979–1995a).

Due Process Versus Collegial Mediation

Most sexual harassment complaints are concluded during the informal stage of the process. Invoking due process at that stage might seriously undermine the efforts at mediation, problem solving, and conciliation that can be effective in a collegial climate. However, particularly when confidentiality is violated, both the person accused and the person bringing a complaint of sexual harassment are potentially at risk. Even unsubstantiated accusations made public may be costly to all involved. In addition, the seriousness of a complaint is not always clear at the start of the process when the parties are not represented by legal counsel. Dilemma: Due process, including legal representation, may undermine the success of mediation during an informal procedure. However, sometimes a matter that seems likely to be resolved during the informal process eventually may require a more serious disciplinary procedure.

A number of procedures restrict due process and the use of an attorney in the early stages. These provisions are made only if expected sanctions are very serious and a disciplinary procedure is required. In these instances, the sexual harassment procedure triggers another disciplinary procedure (for the accused student, faculty, or staff). For example, in the Yale College procedure, if the "complaint is not resolved by the Board or requires action which only the Dean can take, or the complaint needs further investigation or demands more serious sanctions or a formal disciplinary procedure, the complaint will be referred, with further recommendations by the Board, to the Dean of Yale College" (Yale College, 1979–1995a, p. 7). The AAUP procedures provide for a grievance officer to informally effect a mutually acceptable resolution. However, if a faculty committee's findings do not lead to a mutually accepted resolution and if the committee sees reasonable cause for seeking sanctions, the grievance officer forwards the recommendation to the chief administrative officer, who may institute a proceeding to impose a sanction according to the "Recommended Institutional Regulations on Academic Freedom and Tenure," which provides for legal counsel (AAUP, 1995).

Table 4.1 presents an approach based on the severity of a complaint for matching misconduct, sanction, and grievance procedure. In this construction representation by counsel is not an option for instances of sexual harassment that are designated as "minor" but is an option for serious misconduct and sanctions during a full hearing, which may be part of a disciplinary procedure (J. Mingle, personal communication, December 1995).

The vast majority of sexual harassment complaints are reported and resolved in the informal stage of the procedure. Instituting legal representation at that stage is likely to create an adversarial situation that would escalate the matter and reduce the likelihood of successful mediation and problem solving. There are high risks to both the person bringing a sexual harassment complaint and the person accused. It is important for a procedure to be symmetrical and evenhanded in protecting the rights of all concerned. I believe this can be accomplished, while

Table 4.1.   Measured Discipline

Matching Offense, Penalty, and Process		
Degree of Misconduct:	*Minor*	*Serious*
Examples:	Hostile environment— no physical touching	Quid pro quo sexual harassment
		Severe hostile environment
Sanction Imposed:	*Minor*	*Serious*
Examples:	Reprimand	Lengthy suspension
	Mandatory counseling	Dismissal
	Denied salary increase	
Process Provided:	*Grievance proceeding*	*Full hearing*
Examples:	Opportunity to contest	Representation by counsel
	Findings plus tell side of story	Confront/cross-examine

postponing due process to later parts of the procedure (formal stage and instances where serious disciplinary actions are being considered).

False Accusations

Public attention to the problem of sexual harassment and the development of special grievance procedures have raised concerns about the possibility of false accusations. The concerns have been heightened by a continuing debate about problems with recovered memories of sexual abuse elicited by faulty counseling techniques and about the testimony of children in sexual abuse cases.

It is difficult to locate data on the authenticity of sexual harassment complaints. Anecdotal evidence suggests that the percentage of false accusations is extremely low. This estimate of actual instances is even lower when one considers the underreporting of sexual harassment complaints. This is not to suggest that all complaints are justified or that misunderstandings, alternative perspectives, and a host of other factors may not explain circumstances that a person labels as sexual harassment.

In a study of sexual abuse, Shakeshaft and Cohan (1995) share the conclusion that "false allegations constitute only a small percentage of all allegations" (p. 514). They report that only 7.5% of the 225 school superintendents interviewed suggest that some allegations of sexual abuse were untrue or not serious enough to be called sexual abuse (Shakeshaft & Cohan, 1995, p. 514). The experience of those, including myself, who receive sexual harassment complaints suggests that it is very trying and difficult to bring a complaint and that few people, if any, make false accusations. The conclusion that false accusations were rare, was shared by some 25 grievance officers during one of the workshops I led on sexual harassment (Board of Cooperative Educational Services of Nassau County, personal communication, February 10, 1993). However, one grievance officer described an instance where a group of early adolescent girls brought a sexual harassment complaint against a handsome new teacher, which did not appear to be authentic. She speculated and others agreed that false accusations might be more likely from a group of students of junior high school age. I also have heard of one instance in the past 19 years of work in postsecondary institutions where a student bringing a sexual harassment complaint was alleged to have confided in someone that she was bringing the complaint as a way to discredit a faculty member who was about to accuse her of some unrelated unethical behavior.

The debate continues about evidence of child sexual abuse and appropriate approaches to therapy designed to recover hidden or delayed memory. Research has raised awareness of the frequency and detrimental impact of child sexual abuse. This abuse, including incest and nonrelative abuse, may be suffered by as many as 38% of females and 16% of males (Enns, McNeilly, Corkery, & Gilbert, 1995). Some survivors are tormented continuously by memories of child sexual abuse, while others recover these memories, alone or with assistance. However, other individuals may have "iatrogenic" illusory memories and beliefs of child sexual abuse that did not actually happen (Lindsay, 1995). Unfortunately, the eagerness of some mental health professionals to address the problem of sexual abuse sometimes leads to their use of risky memory recovery techniques and to mislabeling of illusory memories.

While the possibility of illusory memory is considerably less frequent than the memories of actual survivors, the possibility of a mistake is of concern. One has to use good judgment and to "develop low-risk ways of working with clients that lead to near-perfect identification of survivors of child sexual abuse" (Lindsay, 1995, p. 288). As we uphold the rights of persons bringing a complaint, we also must protect the rights of a person accused of sexual harassment.

Off-Campus Programs and Activities*

Institutions are responsible for having grievance procedures and for preventing sexual harassment and sexual discrimination in off-campus programs, but are not required to have joint procedures with the field settings. It is important to make provision for this responsibility within the school's procedures. The experience of schools of education and affiliated K–12 off-campus field settings is described to illustrate the issues involved. These issues pertain to all educational institutions that place students in off-campus programs and activities. The issues will be of increasing importance with the expansion of school-to-work education. (See Chapter 2 for discussion of related legal issues and Chapter 6 for educational strategies.)

As yet, there seems to be no systematic survey of schools of education and K–12 schools to determine the existence and nature of sexual harassment policies and grievance procedures, including joint procedures. Based on anecdotal evidence and a limited inquiry, it appears that joint procedures are rare if they exist at all. For example, a number of programs that offer field placements (teacher preparation, psychology) reported that the issue of sexual harassment had not yet been discussed routinely with personnel at the field placement sites (Brandenburg,

---

*Portions of this information have been published in Brandenburg (1995).

1994b). Institutions still seem to be struggling to define sexual harassment and their individual institutional responsibility. Such institutional responsibility might be perceived as even more daunting if it necessitated joint policies with personnel at field placements. It is possible for institutions to consider their joint responsibility without establishing joint procedures. It would be unfortunate if such consideration were delayed until a serious sexual harassment complaint was made by a student at a field placement.

Establishing joint procedures might be difficult. For example, a school of education and the K–12 school or community clinic that serves as a field placement have different constituencies and may be subject to different regulations. Some of the larger schools of education might have difficulty negotiating joint procedures given the large number of off-campus settings they use. Rather than developing joint procedures with each field placement site, it might be wiser and more efficient for the school of education to include issues of sexual harassment at field placements in its own institutional policies and procedures. In addition, the school of education should consult with the field placements about joint interests regarding the problem of sexual harassment.

The school of education may play a vital role in ensuring the development and effectiveness of sexual harassment procedures in its own institution, as well as in the off-campus institutions where its students are placed. It is important, however, that the school of education stay within the university grievance procedures and that any specialized procedures for its program be integrated into the overall university model. Creating separate procedures might be confusing and serve to increase school liability. Any change in procedures should be checked with the university and school counsel. In other words, it is suggested that the school of education first ensure that its own institutional procedures are in place and are effective, and then work with cooperating institutions to develop a shared understanding of the policies and procedures to be followed in the event of a complaint that includes both institutions. The school of education should work with each field placement site to encourage familiarity with the policies and procedures of both institutions and to develop protocols of communication to respond to complaints. In instances where shared procedures are possible, they might follow the model of university-wide procedures developed at some institutions, where the grievance board or panel is composed of various constituencies depending on who is involved in the complaint (K–12 teachers or students, school of education, faculty or administrators, etc.). Unfortunately, this model would be more difficult when institutions are not part of the same organizational entity.

CONCLUSION

All schools, from prekindergarten to universities, and work settings should have written policies and procedures prohibiting sexual harassment. Schools that receive federal funds are required under Title IX to take steps to prevent sex discrimination and sexual harassment, to provide a nonhostile environment, and to provide a grievance procedure for complaints. It is important that faculty, administrators, students, and staff be informed of these policies and that the policies be perceived as effective and fair.

Many schools are in at least titular compliance with their legal obligation to have policies and grievance procedures prohibiting and responding to complaints of sexual harassment. However, the question becomes whether these policies and procedures are effective and fair. In at least one large private university that has had sexual harassment procedures for many years, students reject these procedures and continue to protest the institution's lack of fairness and of grievance procedures. These protests are a consequence of the community's lack of trust in the existing procedures. Clearly, more needs to be done to establish procedures that are recognized and accepted by the school community.

Lack of an adequate grievance procedure for sexual harassment complaints is in itself a violation of the Title IX regulation. The institution must be responsive in taking timely action, following its policies and procedures, and investigating whenever a complaint is received or harassment is observed or suspected. All members of the campus community need to be aware of the varied behaviors that may constitute sexual harassment in order to identify it as quickly as possible. Without procedures and strict adherence to them, an institution may be alleged to have a hostile environment and tacitly to encourage sexual harassment.

This chapter describes general characteristics that contribute to effective policies and procedures. It describes two models of procedures that rely on a single grievance officer and on a grievance board. The importance of the informal stage of a grievance procedure is explicated. Some difficult dilemmas regarding the use of grievance procedures and the problems of evaluating their effectiveness also are considered. Attention is paid to the special responsibility schools have for prohibiting sexual harassment in off-campus programs and activities.

CHAPTER 5

Educating to Raise Awareness

Strong policies and grievance procedures are necessary but not sufficient in addressing the complex problem of sexual harassment. The requisite multidimensional approach to eliminating this behavior also must include long-term educational strategies. As we saw in Chapter 3 on the origins of sexual harassment, schools inadvertently may reinforce patterns of gender inequality and sexual harassment (AAUW, 1992, 1993; Sadker & Sadker, 1994; Shoop & Hayhow, 1994; Stein, Marshall, & Tropp, 1993). The school structure, pedagogy, and attitudes of teachers, parents, and community all may contribute to subtle or blatant forms of discrimination and to sexual harassment. Although sensational cases in the press have raised awareness, many educators are not yet familiar with the term *sexual harassment* or aware that its underlying behaviors are pervasive and detrimental. It is therefore not surprising that most schools have not developed educational strategies to combat sexual harassment.

> Rose, a three-year-old girl, is in nursery school. One day after class, Mrs. Gardner, the teacher, asks to speak with Rose's mother. The teacher explains that earlier in the school day she found Rose and two three-year-old boys "playing doctor" and that the boys had pulled down Rose's underpants. The teacher advises the mother to dress Rose in pants instead of skirts and to teach her to say "no." The mother asks the teacher what advice she has given to the parents of the two little boys. The teacher replies that she had not thought to speak to the boys' parents. (Strock-Lynskey, 1993)

The case study of Rose is based on an actual occurrence. It suggests how early and deeply rooted are the attitudes and experiences that contribute to the acceptance of sexual harassment. Rose's story illustrates both why it is difficult to address sexual harassment and why educational strategies to combat this behavior are needed at all levels in our schools. (See the suggestions for developing case studies, an important pedagogical approach, later in this chapter.)

As the EEOC (1980) guidelines state, "Prevention is the best tool for the elimination of sexual harassment.'' Education offers our best hope for prevention. Schools at all levels need to educate administrators, faculty, staff, students, and parents about the underlying attitudes of discrimination that permit sexual harassment and about the attitudes of respect that would forestall its occurrence. The links between overt sexual harassment, gender inequity, and sex-role stereotypes must be made clear. Faculty must be encouraged to examine their own attitudes and beliefs as a necessary prerequisite to change. Eliminating sexual harassment through education requires intervention on two levels: (1) broad transformation of climate, curricula, and teaching to eliminate sexual harassment's underlying causes; and (2) specific educational strategies for directly addressing and preventing sexual harassment.

This chapter presents an approach to the broad institutional transformation, and specific strategies to educate about sexual harassment. It includes an overview of what is known about education to change attitudes and behavior and a general format for direct education to prevent sexual harassment. Case studies based on examples of sexual harassment across educational levels provide a powerful pedagogical approach that can be tailored to all educational settings. Chapter 6 gives more specific suggestions regarding these areas for schools at all levels.

A MODEL ENVIRONMENT

Schools may serve as models of fair and equitable professional standards and take affirmative actions to prevent sexual harassment on campus. The changes must be systemic as well as systematic. Within the school, the understanding starts with self-examination of attitudes and actions and extends to an examination of policies, practices, and climate. Central to the task is a review of classroom practices and the curricula in all subject areas to eliminate gender bias and to ensure inclusion of scholarship on women and gender. It is essential that the school leadership (administrators and faculty) clearly endorse the importance of these activities and demonstrate commitment to making changes that will eliminate gender bias and sexual harassment. The institution must develop and publicize a strong policy prohibiting sexual harassment and institute grievance procedures for hearing and handling complaints. Counseling and advisement about sexual harassment should be made available. The community must be educated and information about the issue disseminated on an ongoing basis. Inservice workshops, courses, and speakers on sexual harassment may serve to encourage and assist teachers and school personnel. Workshops should be directed at all members of the school community, including students, faculty, administrators, and other personnel, such as bus drivers, janitors, and food service workers. An atmosphere of sensitivity, respect, and understanding must be created.

As an example, at Teachers College, Columbia University, efforts began with an institutional statement declaring that harassment of any nature, and specifically sexual harassment, had no place in that community. More than a year was spent with representatives of the college community developing new policies and procedures that reflected the value position, including formally defining sexual harassment and establishing a panel to hear and resolve grievances. Educational opportunities were provided for supervisors, employees, faculty, and students to learn about the entrenched attitudes underlying sexual harassment and how to address them. As part of these educational efforts, a series of seminars and workshops was held on the topic of sexual harassment. Participants included members of the faculty, staff, and students at the College, as well as human resource specialists from other institutions. A faculty seminar on the scholarship on women and gender and the implications for curricula, started in 1985, continued into its ninth year. Discussion of these issues was initiated with the Teacher Education Policy Committee, which represents all teacher preparation programs at the college. Sexual harassment was identified by the dean as one of the priority areas for student research. Dean's grants were made to several students for research on these issues. Surveys to determine patterns of behavior and sexual harassment are being considered by the grievance board. Funds are being sought to support faculty engaged in curriculum review. The implications for student teachers, counseling interns, and all off-campus placements are being reviewed. Much more needs to be done, including an evaluation of the effectiveness of these efforts.

IMPLEMENTING EDUCATIONAL STRATEGIES TO CHANGE ATTITUDES AND BEHAVIOR

Education to prevent sexual harassment will require changing attitudes and behavior. While there are a growing number of educational interventions that address sexual harassment (Stein & Sjostrom, 1994; Strauss & Espeland, 1992), there is as yet little research on the effectiveness of such programs (Fitzgerald & Shullman, 1993). In the meantime, studies that have been completed on attitude and behavior change and on changing racial attitudes may be informative and suggest the components of effective educational interventions to change attitudes about sexual harassment. These studies suggest that education directed at counteracting sex-role stereotypes and raising awareness about sexual harassment can change attitudes and behavior.

The relationship between attitudes and behaviors is not completely understood and far from simple. A meta-analysis reveals a robust connection between attitudes and behavior (Kim & Hunter, 1993). The research illustrates how changing behavior may lead to attitude change (Bem, 1968; Festinger, 1957) and how changing attitudes can change behavior (Calder & Ross, 1973; Fishbein & Ajzen, 1975). Persuasive communication can demonstrably influence attitudes and behavior (Calder & Ross, 1973, Fishbein & Ajzen, 1975; Kim & Hunter, 1993). We may extract from these studies the principles that will produce effective workshops and educational interventions. (See components of educational interventions in the next section.)

The potential effectiveness of educational interventions to change sexual harassment attitudes may be inferred from studies on changing racial attitudes. Overall, the effectiveness of interracial contact and cooperative-learning interventions on reducing prejudiced attitudes is well supported (Banks, 1995; Barnard & Benn, 1988; Weigel, Weiser, & Cook, 1975). An analysis of educational interventions found both cognitive and affective treatments to be effective in changing attitudes toward ethnic minority groups. Affective interventions, which involved interracial contact, had the greatest impact on decreasing the perceived social distance and increasing positive attitudes (Furuto & Furuto, 1983). A popular prejudice-reduction simulation, "Brown-Eyes-Blue-Eyes," has subjects participate in an environment that discriminates against those with blue eyes. The majority of participants report that they find the experience personally meaningful, while moderate support is found for the general effectiveness of the approach (Byrnes & Kiger, 1990).

Encouragement for the use of education to change behavior, in this case sexual harassment, can be gleaned from the success of a variety of behavior change programs dealing with issues such as sexuality, sexism, and drug use that have proven effective (Gross, 1994; Howard & McCabe, 1990; Schonfeld et al., 1995). The success of programs like Weight Watchers and Alcoholics Anonymous bears testimony to the success of changing attitudes and behaviors. There are also a variety of popular programs addressing sexuality and sex equity that appear promising but have not yet been evaluated (DeSpelder & Strickland, 1982; Wilson & Kirby, 1984; Wisconsin Department of Public Instruction, 1993). Often prompted by court rulings on discrimination and the requirements of affirmative action, many corporations, including AT&T, offer workshops or classes on pluralism that include educational components on sexism and racism. Data on formal evaluation of these programs are scant. However, anecdotal reports by the corporations attest to their success in bringing about some change (Kilborn, 1995).

While the press tends to report that programs are highly successful and promising, the research literature evaluating educational programs is somewhat more mixed (De Gaston, Jensen, Weed, & Tanas, 1994; Harrison, Downes, & Williams, 1991; Visser & Van Bilsen, 1994). The majority of sex education programs are found to affect knowledge and, to a lesser extent, attitudes; however, most do not affect behavior, with the important exception of those that target contraception use (De Gaston et al., 1994; Harrison et al., 1991; Visser & Van Bilsen, 1994). An evaluation, including a measure of intention to have sex, of abstinence-focused sex education programs implemented in four states found attitude change. Greater change took place when teachers were supportive of the program's objectives (De Gaston et al., 1994). The importance of teacher involvement also is stressed by Moore, Waguespack, Wickstrom, Witt, and Gaydos (1994), who state that to be acceptable to teachers, interventions must attend to the time and resources demanded and the complexity of the program. A program on AIDS education for elementary school children produced better conceptual understanding of the disease and decreased misperceptions, and the knowledge was proven to be retained in a follow-up procedure (Schonfeld et al., 1995).

Several programs have had an impact on behavior as well as attitudes. The Postponing Sexual Involvement for Young Teens Program is a highly successful educational program. A 5-year study of more than 500 students showed that program completers were more than four times less likely to become sexually involved than non-program students (Howard & McCabe, 1990). A drug intervention studied by Cornell University Medical College was demonstrated to have long-term effects on reducing drug use (Botvin, Baker, Dugenbury, Botvin, & Diaz, 1995).

Insight into the likely success of programs to prevent sexual harassment may be gleaned from a review of programs that target attitudes and behaviors surrounding sexual aggression. A few studies have sought to change attitudes pertaining to rape and sexual harassment. In one study of 821 university students on the effects of an educational intervention on date rape, women were found to be more likely than men to significantly change their rape-supportive attitudes (Lenihan, Rawlins, Eberly, Buckley, & Masters, 1992). Another date rape intervention was found to significantly alter men's but not women's attitudes (Harrison et al., 1991). A study designed to assess the effectiveness of a workshop aimed at changing sexual harassment attitudes found significant attitude change in resident advisors (male and female) and demonstrated that such programs can be successful (Beauvais, 1986).

Exposure to educational material regarding sexual inequality resulted in all subjects viewing rape victims more favorably, with males reporting less likelihood to commit rape (Johnson & Russ, 1989). Similarly, an intervention using didactic and experiential approaches that targeted sexual aggression-supportive attitudes was found to affect immediate and long-term attitude change and to have an impact on behavior (Gilbert, Heesacker, & Gannon, 1991). A follow-up study supported these results, found this intervention effective with students holding traditional sex-role attitudes, and produced attitude change that endured for at least one month following treatment (Rosenthal, Heesacker, & Neimeyer, 1995).

COMPONENTS OF AN EDUCATIONAL
INTERVENTION ON SEXUAL HARASSMENT

The above studies include components that should be considered in developing an effective educational intervention on sexual harassment.

1. Discuss sex roles and gender stereotypes (consciousness raising) (Johnson & Russ, 1989).
   - Reflect on the influence of sex roles in daily life.
   - Consider myths about women, men, and their social and sexual interaction, and the origins of behaviors that are experienced as harassing (Gilbert et al., 1991; Harrison et al., 1991; Lee, 1987; Sandberg, et al., 1987).
   - Examine power dynamics, including the power given to men by virtue of their gender and other less obvious forms (Carr, 1991; Paludi, 1990; Zalk, 1990).
2. Target specific behaviors (Fishbein & Ajzen, 1975).
3. Target beliefs acceptable to the audience (Fishbein & Ajzen, 1975).
4. Engage participants in perspective taking, using role playing, and active participation (Fishbein & Ajzen, 1975).
   - Use role playing as performing in a novel role to bring about understanding (Bem, 1968; Calder & Ross, 1973; Festinger, 1957).
5. Provide assertiveness training and develop communication skills (Sandberg et al., 1987).

6. Engage leaders who are likable, high status, trustworthy, and convey an understandable message (Fishbein & Ajzen, 1975).
7. Encourage teacher involvement and support (De Gaston et al., 1994; Moore et al., 1994).
8. Counteract events that may intervene between intention and behavior (e.g., peer pressure, counter messages in environment). Create supportive environment in school (Calder & Ross, 1973; Fishbein & Ajzen, 1975).
9. Provide solid information on definitions and examples, incidence of sexual harassment, sexual assault, and referral sources.

Workshops and Presentations on Sexual Harassment

Individual schools may build on the work discussed above and follow the general format of a workshop or presentation on sexual harassment, as described below. The format can be adapted to the specific audience, including students, inservice or preservice teachers, administrators, counselors, teacher and counselor educators, parents, school staff, and the general public. Incoming students, faculty, and staff, as well as continuing members of the school community, should receive periodic training about the issue of sexual harassment.

Workshops to prevent and respond to sexual harassment might include the following 10 components:

1. Define sexual harassment and provide information on its incidence. Present general information about sexual harassment in educational institutions and the workplace.
2. Describe both obvious and subtle behaviors that constitute sexual harassment. Give examples that include quid pro quo and hostile environment harassment (forced kissing, pulling someone's clothes off, making sexual remarks in jest, name calling, etc.).
3. Review relevant legislation, administrative proceedings, and important legal cases. Summarize the provisions of Title VII and Title IX.
4. Review sexual harassment policies and grievance procedures in place at the school and used at other educational institutions. Explain how they work.
5. Consider the roots of sexual harassment:
   a) development of sex roles and gender identity;
   b) sexism, gender inequity, and the unequal distribution of

power (discuss social norms, values, attitudes, and practices that permit discriminatory behaviors to continue);

c) interpersonal issues relevant to the specific audience.

6. Use case studies. Learn to identify sexual harassment. Use perspective taking. Use reflection—offer an opportunity for participants to examine their own attitudes, values, and beliefs about
sexual harassment.

7. Include issues specific to the audience (e.g., for students likely
to sexually harass). Work on dispelling rape myths and adversarial sexual beliefs and help participants learn to take on someone else's perspective as a means of reducing the likelihood to
sexually harass (Pryor, 1987).

8. Suggest strategies for responding to and preventing sexual harassment. Include proactive and responsive strategies, such as
role play, peer education, assertiveness training, communication skill development, and support groups.

9. Consider approaches to developing educational interventions—review of curricula, model units of curriculum transformation, and AAUW recommendations for changing climate
(AAUW, 1992).

10. Provide resources—model sexual harassment curricula, grievance procedures, policies and educational interventions, posters, audiovisuals, organizations, and referral sources.

The content of educational workshops and presentations will have
to be updated regularly to keep participants abreast of legal and educational developments. Institutions will benefit by consulting regularly
with their legal advisors to stay informed of their responsibilities. Institutions should conduct training sessions at least once a year for new staff
and inservice personnel.

CASE STUDIES FOR EDUCATING TO
PREVENT SEXUAL HARASSMENT

Case studies are a very important pedagogical tool in educating
about sexual harassment. The following case studies are based on a
variety of sources: experiences of a sexual harassment grievance board;
communications from administrators, faculty, and students; publications; private conversations; and public discussions. They reflect instances of sexual harassment that have occurred in educational settings

at all levels. These case studies may be adopted for a variety of educational purposes. They might be included in a sexual harassment workshop for school personnel and members of the community or used in the preparation of counselors, teachers, and health providers. One or more of the case studies may be presented and discussion among the participants stimulated with questions like the ones that follow each vignette. The participants should be encouraged to examine their assumptions, reactions, and judgments. They should try to adopt the viewpoint of each of the parties involved in the case. Participants should try to imagine the same situations with all possible gender and role combinations (e.g., female harassed by male, male harassed by female, male harassed by male, female harassed by female, student harassed by teacher, or teacher harassed by student). They also should try to distinguish among claims of sexual harassment that are legitimate, based on misunderstanding, or contrived. Case study features include power, gender, cross-cultural differences, and the context of the academic or work setting.

Pre-Kindergarten

Consider the example of Rose, documented at the beginning of this chapter.

1. Has Rose been sexually harassed?
2. Where is the line between exploration, appropriate social interaction, and sexual harassment?
3. What attitudes or beliefs does the teacher bring to this situation?
4. In what ways might these attitudes actually contribute to sexual harassment?
5. How do we help the teacher to examine the responsibilities of the boys, of Rose, and of their families?

K–12 Cases

Student/Student

Vivian, a first-year high school student, has had very little experience dating. When she walks down the halls in school, boys often stare at her, but she tries to ignore them. One boy, Ted, stands outside her homeroom every day and regularly makes suggestive comments. Although Vivian feels annoyed and offended, she shrugs off her embarrassment by giggling and turning away, because she doesn't know what else to do. Ted is encouraged by what he thinks is Vivian's interest in him. He calls and asks her out. Vivian isn't interested, but she doesn't know how to say no without hurting his feelings. She's also scared of getting a reputation for being cold. She cuts the conversation short by agreeing to meet him. Ted is pleased that he might be getting somewhere. Vivian is worried.

The next day Vivian has second thoughts about the date and cuts her last class to avoid being around after school. As she is leaving, Ted spots her down the hall and runs after her. Vivian sees him coming and ducks into an empty classroom, feeling foolish and scared. Ted catches up to her and corners her in the room. Before she can get away, he grabs her, saying, "Where are you going?" "Help!" Vivian shouts. Ted says, "What's the matter with you? I thought that you wanted to see me!" Vivian screams "No!" and runs out of the school (Klein & Wilber, 1986).

1. Should this case be handled as sexual harassment?
2. How, if at all, should the school intervene?
3. How well founded were Vivian's fears?
4. How might schools prevent this kind of situation?

Student/Student

In a high school English class, sucking and kissing sounds come from behind Lisa. The sounds turn to moaning and grunting, and she turns around to ask the boys to stop. John stops long enough to comment on her breasts, eliciting giggles from his buddies. The teacher asks Lisa about the poem that he just read, and she is forced to confess that she missed it. On the way out, John tells her he'll see her in his wet dreams.

Lisa's guidance counselor notices her falling grades. After an assembly on sexual harassment, she also notices that the girl is visibly upset, and pulls her aside. In her office, she presses Lisa, who finally begins to cry and admits that some of what she saw in the assembly was happening to her. She also claims that she has been pushed against the lockers and fondled. She asks the counselor not to tell anyone: She doesn't want anyone to get in trouble. The boy in question is extremely popular and considered a good student.

At the counselor's insistence, Lisa writes a letter to John, explaining how cheap and frightened his actions make her feel. The counselor explains that no one will get in trouble, but that any further complaints will be followed by action. She asks Lisa to let her deliver the letter, and

Lisa refuses, stating that she is scared of what the boys might do to her (Miller, 1993).

1. What, if anything, should the counselor do?
2. How realistic are Lisa's fears of retaliation?
3. What are the school's legal and ethical responsibilities regarding the students involved in this case?
4. Are there problems with the school's policy on sexual harassment?

Student/Teacher

A veteran teacher witnesses Mr. Wright, a new teacher, giving a quick hug to one of his female students. A few days later, she sees the same student embrace Mr. Wright and kiss him on the cheek. Although no one has complained about the new teacher—in fact, he seems very popular with his students—these displays of affection make the witness uneasy. She goes to the principal and reports that Mr. Wright is being inappropriately affectionate with one of his students. The principal calls Mr. Wright to her office and relays the complaint. Mr. Wright explains that such displays of affection are a common part of the culture that he and the student share. The student verifies that Mr. Wright's behavior was not a problem and was culturally appropriate.

1. Is this sexual harassment? Inappropriate behavior?
2. Should the school intervene?
3. How might others at the school, such as the teacher who reported the incident, and other students respond when they witness similar incidents?
4. What is the school's responsibility to third parties who may be disturbed by Mr. Wright's behavior?

Students on the Job/Manager

Mr. Wilson is branch manager of a bank that has seven tellers, two of whom are male work-study trainees from the local high school. Periodically, he visits each of the teller cages to supervise transactions. Whenever he visits the area assigned to the work-study students, he frequently touches them, puts his arm around them when giving individual instruction, and pats one of them on his way out. Neither of the students has rebuffed his actions or complained to him directly. He has never asked either of them for sexual favors (Minnesota Department of Education, 1993).

1. Is Mr. Wilson's behavior sexual harassment?
2. What are the bank's legal and ethical responsibilities to both the manager and the students?
3. What are the high school's legal and ethical responsibilities?
4. How can the school educate personnel at the off-campus placement?

Junior High School Students/Student Teacher

Ms. Blank, a degree candidate in a department of teacher education, has been placed in a local public junior high school for student teaching. She befriends her students by meeting them after class and taking an interest in their after-school activities and problems. She repeatedly sends personal notes and poems to three of the students. This behavior is called to the attention of some of the teachers at the school, and a cooperating teacher reports what is deemed inappropriate behavior to the student teacher's supervisor at the school of education. When questioned by her supervisor, Ms. Blank denies that her behavior is inappropriate.

1. Is this an instance of sexual harassment?
2. What are the school of education's responsibilities regarding the student teacher and the three junior high students?
3. What are the junior high school's responsibilities in this case?
4. If one of the students filed a complaint, what grievance procedure would be used?
5. How might the school of education and the junior high cooperate to respond?

Teacher/Assistant Principal

Ms. Green, a young teacher who has been teaching part time for several years, takes her exam and gets her license. For the first 3 years at her new teaching position, she will be on probation before being awarded tenure. Six months before the tenure review, Mr. Lee, the assistant principal, schedules a teaching observation. In the private meeting that follows, he sits virtually on top of her. She is very uncomfortable. At their next meeting, she determines to let Mr. Lee sit down first so that she can sit at a comfortable distance. He tells her to come closer and she refuses.

The visits occur with increasing frequency, and without warning, and for the first time, he starts giving her unsatisfactory comments on the observations. Mr. Lee also transfers problem students into Ms. Green's class, effectively lowering the average grade level of her class.

Ms. Green discusses the situation with fellow teachers, who suggest that the assistant principal is "dangerous" and advise against reporting to the principal since he and Mr. Lee are close friends.

1. Is Mr. Lee's behavior sexual harassment?
2. What advice would you give the teacher?
3. What are the considerations for and against making a complaint?
4. What might be done to address this situation?

Higher Education Cases

Undergraduate/Teaching Assistant

Jane, a graduate student teaching assistant, sends notes and propositions to Bill, one of the undergraduates in her class, and then asks him to meet for advisement during the late evening. Bill is upset, and even more embarrassed because when he tells his friends they do not see this as a problem and advise him to "go for it" with the teaching assistant. Nobody seems to understand Bill's confusion, embarrassment, and feelings of inadequacy.

1. Is this sexual harassment?
2. What, if any, are the implications of the harasser being female and the victim male?
3. If he were to complain, what special difficulties (if any) might he face because of his gender?

Undergraduate/Teaching Assistant

Kim, a 20-year-old undergraduate, is taking a large lecture course in which a graduate student, Jeff, age 23, is a teaching assistant. Jeff begins approaching her after class and making light conversation. Over several weeks, he becomes increasingly personal, asking her intimate questions and eventually asking her out. Throughout, Kim has been polite and friendly, but she is increasingly upset at the advances. She has told no one. After making an excuse to avoid going out with Jeff, she files a complaint with the designated convener of the sexual harassment board.

Two members of the grievance board make an appointment with Jeff, but he fails to show up. Another appointment is scheduled, and he arrives terribly upset. He appears very anxious and unsure of himself. It quickly becomes apparent that Jeff is confused about the whole incident. The board members describe Kim's feelings of powerlessness, anxiety, and fear for her grade. Jeff appears truly surprised, as Kim has never conveyed her discomfort to him and he is a lonely graduate student who doesn't experience himself as someone with power.

1. Is Jeff's behavior sexual harassment or innocent flirting?
2. How should the members of the grievance board handle the situation?
3. What might the college do to avoid this kind of situation in the future?

Faculty/Student

Ms. Young, a history teacher, is visited by Joe, a student athlete who is dressed only in running shorts. In addition to revealing his body, Joe says that he is attracted to Ms. Young and asks if she can give him "special help" with his senior thesis. Joe calls Ms. Young continually.

1. Is this sexual harassment? Contrapower harassment?
2. How might Ms. Young respond?
3. Does the school bear any responsibility for Joe's behavior?
4. What might the school do to forestall actions like Joe's in the future?

Counseling Intern/Director of Counseling

Ms. King, a graduate student in counseling psychology, is fulfilling her internship at a community mental health clinic. When she first started at the clinic she was interviewed by Dr. Brown, the Director of Counseling, who was very friendly and shared personal experiences with her, including that he had recently been divorced. The meeting ended with Dr. Brown's welcoming Ms. King to the clinic and giving her a hug. Although in retrospect the interaction makes Ms. King uncomfortable, at the time she did not give it much thought.

Since then whenever Ms. King runs into Dr. Brown at the clinic, he hugs her and behaves affectionately. She finds his behavior increasingly inappropriate and becomes more and more uncomfortable. Eventually, he asks her out. The student intern reports her discomfort at this invitation to her graduate school supervisor but indicates that she hopes for a job in the clinic and is fearful of taking any action.

After a time, and with the support of her supervisor, Ms. King tells the director that his behavior makes her uncomfortable and asks him to stop. The student intern's supervisor also speaks to Dr. Brown. The director responds that he is being misinterpreted. He suggests it is his style to be personal in communicating with colleagues. Furthermore, he suggests that Ms. King appeared to reciprocate his personal interest.

1. Is this sexual harassment?
2. What are the clinic's legal and ethical responsibilities to the student intern?
3. What are the graduate school's responsibilities to the student intern?
4. What can the clinic and the graduate school do to avoid this type of situation?

Faculty/Student

A student and a faculty member are in a consensual romantic relationship. One wants to end the relationship and the other doesn't.

1. Is there a threat or penalty for ending the relationship if the student breaks it off? If the faculty member ends it? What if the faculty member is the only doctoral advisor in the student's area of interest?
2. How do third parties feel when this intimate relationship is going on?
3. What is the school's responsibility, if any?
4. Would the gender of the two participants make any difference in your opinion of the case?

Undergraduate/Faculty

Professor Olds, a faculty member at an undergraduate institution, agrees to meet with students in his office to work on class materials for a difficult science course. He makes appointments with some students for Saturdays, when the office building is usually vacant. One of the students, John, accuses Professor Olds of making sexual advances when he goes to his office for help. Word of his accusation quickly spreads throughout the campus, and soon two additional students come forward to claim that they also have been harassed. A few weeks later, after a university investigation that does not include interviewing Professor Olds, he is dismissed from the faculty.

1. Was this an instance of sexual harassment?
2. Were the institution's actions fair?
3. What procedures should have been followed?
4. What impact might these events have on Professor Olds and on the undergraduate institution?

Undergraduate/Coach

Ms. White, the women's tennis coach, becomes very close to the members of the girls' varsity tennis team. She is quite physical and affectionate with June, the team captain. June is very uncomfortable with Ms. White's repeated invitations to her home.

1. Is this sexual harassment?
2. How should June respond?
3. What sexual harassment policy should exist?
4. What action, if any, should the college take?

Student/Student

A male and a female student spend a long evening together at a sorority keg party. They drink a lot and at her insistence wind up going to her room where they have sex. The next day, she reports having a great time, and he is embarrassed; he doesn't remember how he got there since he has a regular girlfriend.

1. Is this sexual harassment?
2. How can the experiences of the two students be understood?
3. What role does gender play in understanding this situation?

Suggestions for Case Study Development

In tailoring case study examples to a group, one might consider some additional situations, developing appropriate questions to elicit self-examination, courses of action, educational interventions, and discussion.

- A student client has a sexual relationship with her psychologist in the school counseling center.
- Two students complain about a campus minister. The minister frequently touches students and calls them late at night. He claims this is just his pastoral approach.
- A high school student football captain persistently asks out the student teacher in his biology class.
- Two undergraduate students on a date are "making out." After hours of heavy petting they eventually have intercourse. He thinks it was consensual. She wakes up the next day and declares that she has been raped.
- On the school bus, sixth-grade boys tease a fifth-grade girl about her breasts.
- A group of female teacher preparation students stare and send sexual notes to one of the few male students in the preservice program.

CONCLUSION

The links between sexual harassment and attitudes about gender and sex roles suggest approaches to intervening and preventing sexual harassment. Attitudes and behaviors can be changed through education. It would be preferable to have a clear and tested approach to education regarding sexual harassment. Unfortunately, while some efforts have been made to educate about sexual harassment, data on their effectiveness are scant. In the meantime, we can extrapolate from what we know about changing behavior and attitudes through educational interventions in other areas, including rape prevention, sex education, and sexism and racism. Some components of effective interventions are suggested here and in the following chapter.

For school change to be effective, it must be systemic and involve the entire community, as well as systematic and include a comprehensive approach. The change must involve the school climate and curricula, establish clear sexual harassment policies and procedures, and include specific educational programs targeted to prevent sexual harassment.

Case studies based on actual instances of sexual harassment may be used in a variety of educational experiences from workshops to preparation programs for educators. Cases include issues of power, gender, cultural differences, and the academic and work settings. Each institution may develop its own case studies adapted to the particular audiences, purposes, and educational context.

CHAPTER 6

Developing Educational Strategies

Education to prevent sexual harassment requires an institutional commitment, transformation of climate and curricula, and the development of educational strategies. This chapter continues to make the case for the need to address sexual harassment at each educational level. The sections that follow provide suggestions and examples of educational opportunities and strategies that may be developed for higher education, schools of education, and middle, secondary, and elementary school settings. Because of the special responsibility of schools of education, I include a separate section on them and on preparation programs for teachers, counselors, and administrators. The concluding section discusses considerations for educating parents and involving them in the elimination of sexual harassment. Resources for this work by schools at all levels and for parent education are found in Appendix B.

HIGHER EDUCATION

The issue of sexual harassment was identified at colleges and universities in the late 1970s. Since that time, although many institutions have taken some steps to prevent its occurrence, the number of sexual harassment complaints has increased (Lewin, 1995; "Sexual Harassment Suits on the Rise," 1994; U.S. Department of Education, 1993). Educators should consider why flagrant as well as subtle instances of sexual harassment continue, and how attitudes and values may prevent the recognition and questioning of sexual harassment. Additional efforts that emphasize educational strategies are required.

A survey of 11 research universities with schools of education in New York State gives a sense of what institutions of higher education are doing about sexual harassment (Brandenburg, 1994a).

- *Policies and Procedures*: All schools surveyed have formal policies and procedures prohibiting sexual harassment as required by Title IX. The effectiveness of these procedures typically is ranked as "moderate." Most respondents (64%) hear sexual harassment complaints as part of a single grievance procedure that receives complaints of several types of discrimination. Others (36%) have a separate procedure exclusively for sexual harassment complaints. The grievance procedures involve a grievance officer in 80% of schools and a grievance board in 20% of schools.

- *Complaints*: Participating institutions receive an average of 5 formal and 10 informal complaints of sexual harassment a year (range: formal 0–15, informal 1–25). Formal complaints include 44% student versus faculty, 21% staff versus staff, 19% student versus student, and 16% other. Typically, informal complaints involve more peer harassment, as discussed in Chapter 1. Half of the participants report that legal action has been taken against their institutions for sexual harassment.
- *Curriculum*: Few curricular efforts have been designed to address sexual harassment. The issue sometimes is included in a course on "women's issues" that is offered through a women's studies program, or in a workshop on sexual harassment presented to undergraduates. However, the issue of sexual harassment rarely is included elsewhere in the school curricula.
- *Publicity*: Participating institutions use a number of methods to publicize sexual harassment policies and grievance procedures, as follows: 64% distribute a brochure or flyer, 45% send a mailing annually to students and faculty, and 36% include information in faculty and student handbooks. Seventy three percent use more than one of the above methods to publicize policies and procedures.
- *Significance*: Sexual harassment is considered to be a "moderate" problem at these institutions. Respondents suggest that the issue of sexual harassment is "very important" and that educational institutions need assistance in responding to this issue. They indicate that it is "very important" that educational interventions be developed to address sexual harassment.

Additional methods used by colleges to increase awareness of sexual harassment include dissemination of information through notices in student newspapers, posters, and radio spots; special workshops and orientation sessions; brown-bag lunches; peer educators; expert speakers; and sexual harassment as a topic for general and departmental meetings (Bohmer & Parrot, 1993; Goodwin, Roscoe, Rose, & Repp, 1989; McCormick, Adams-Bohley, Peterson, & Gaeddert, 1989; Paludi, 1990).

A number of institutions include workshops on sexual harassment for incoming students, teaching assistants, faculty, and staff. Antioch College in Yellow Springs, Ohio, mandates that first-year students attend sexual consent workshops as part of orientation. First-year student orientation at Columbia College, Columbia University, includes forums on homosexuality and date rape (Gross, 1993b; Rothstein, 1992). St. Cloud State University required that all new first-year students in fall 1992 attend a 2-hour session on sexual assault. Those who did not attend were not allowed to register for the winter quarter (Higher Education Coordinating Board & Office of the Attorney General, Minnesota, 1993).

Some colleges and universities involve their students as peer educators. Upperclass students at Antioch College help conduct sexual consent workshops (Gross, 1993b), and Lehigh University has a student group that educates about acquaintance rape (Celis, 1991). Students have organized candlelight walks and "Take Back the Night" marches at campuses across the country to fight rape and sexual abuse (Celis, 1991; Gross, 1993b).

The military continues to experience a high incidence of sexual harassment as it includes women in more areas (Murduch & Nichol, 1995). The Air Force Academy in Colorado Springs responded to sexual harassment complaints from female cadets with the following wide-ranging institutional measures:

1. Court-martialing and jailing an instructor and a cadet for sexual misconduct
2. Disciplining three cadets, and requiring the resignation of three others
3. Establishing a 24-hour confidential special telephone number to report sexual assaults
4. Holding a 4-hour confidential session in which the women cadets talked about sexual harassment on campus with the superintendent of the Academy, followed by a session with the male cadets
5. Recognizing the issue of climate—although 50% of the women cadets knew of sexual harassment cases, only 9% of the men did
6. Creating a Center for Character Development, where ethics, honor code, and human relations will be taught in an integrated manner
7. Offering a new course—Gender, Race, and Human Dignity
8. Developing a new training program for faculty to help them recognize and prevent sexual harassment
9. Developing skits on date rape for incoming first-year students to watch

10. Implementing a crash course in "human relations" to heighten sensitivity and increase awareness (Schmitt, 1994, pp. 1, 34)

Most higher education institutions have established sexual harassment policies and grievance procedures but few have developed educational strategies. Unfortunately, there has not been a systematic study of the effectiveness of these efforts. Institutions of higher education are encouraged to consider the strategies described in this chapter as they develop their own approaches geared to their specific needs and context.

SCHOOLS OF EDUCATION

A school of education must be beyond reproach in responding to sexual harassment and should take the lead in uncovering and combating sexist attitudes that allow harassment to continue. As schools of education prepare their students to stop sexual harassment in educational and human service settings, they have a responsibility to serve as model institutions. Schools of education are in a unique position to provide a model environment that is free of sexual harassment, to prepare tomorrow's educational leaders to attend to this issue, and to work with institutions, including their own and off-campus field placements, to eliminate and prevent sexual harassment. Chapter 5 described elements of a model environment, along with an example of the steps taken at one school of education.

Preparing Educational Leaders

Teachers

Unfortunately, the formal curricula of most schools of education remain essentially unchanged by discussion of issues such as sexual harassment, teen pregnancy, and date rape that are taking place in the media, courts, and our communities. A number of educators, including Sadker, Sadker, and Shakeshaft (1987) and Stein and colleagues (1993), have taken the lead in pointing out the disparity between critical social problems like sexual harassment and the content of teacher preparation programs. They suggest that students coming into a teacher preparation program are not given information about sexual harassment and other social problems. While these comments focus on teacher preparation programs, they also are valid for programs to prepare counselors and administrators, which will be discussed at the end of this section.

There is some evidence that change is occurring, and that schools of education are seeking ways to become more responsive to these issues; however, progress is slow. Education to prevent sexual harassment requires a change of current curricula, teaching practice, and teacher education. The work involves re-examination, revision, and inclusion throughout the curricula. This process provides an opportunity for teacher preparation faculty and students working together to explore their attitudes and values, curricula, and school practices regarding the issue of sexual harassment and its underlying causes. Such efforts may lead schools of education to offer courses on the subject of sexual harassment (e.g., child sexual abuse and sexual harassment in schools), to address the issue as part of a general transformation throughout the curricula, or both.

Curricular efforts should be directed at preservice and inservice teachers who learn about preventing and responding to sexual harassment. Areas covered might include

1. Self-examination of personal and community attitudes and values (Why do present school personnel tend to ignore sexual harassment? What attitudes and values might prevent them from recognizing and questioning sexual harassment?)
2. Typical instances of gender bias and sexual harassment among school children
3. Psychosocial determinants of gender discrimination and sexual harassment
4. Curriculum review for bias and to increase representation of women
5. Use of case studies (such as those discussed in Chapter 5) to highlight the complexities of sexual harassment
6. Ethical and legal issues regarding sexual harassment (see Chapter 2)
7. Methods to ensure that K–12 students understand the meaning of sexual harassment and types of behavior involved
8. Methods of intervention to prevent sexual harassment and to respond to instances of sexual harassment
9. Responsibilities in responding to suspected sexual harassment and child abuse

In addition to direct efforts to highlight the problem of sexual harassment, the issue may be considered along with other topics that are important to teacher preparation, such as diversity, sexuality, and textbooks. Sexual harassment may be discussed in the context of fostering understanding and respect among all people and supporting diversity in schools. Sexual harassment shares many characteristics with other forms of discrimination against groups with limited power. Discussions of sexual harassment may be included with the consideration of issues of race, class, and sexual orientation. The development of mutual respect that is critical for preventing sexual harassment has implications for eliminating all types of discrimination.

Sexual harassment is partly an issue of power and partly an issue with a manifest sexual component. As institutions design educational interventions and programs to prevent sexual harassment, it is necessary to consider the strong feelings and taboos associated with sexuality. It is important to acknowledge the difficulty many people experience in dealing with the intimate nature of the topic and the associated moral, religious, and personal values. As we learn more about the high incidence of incest and child sexual abuse, we further appreciate the difficulties associated with addressing this topic. School personnel and parents will need assistance in considering sexual matters and related attitudes regarding their children. In spite of the difficulties, courses on sexual harassment and child sexual abuse are needed to support educators and parents in fulfilling their responsibility to report and prevent such behavior.

As the writers and selectors of textbooks, faculty members and students of schools of education bear a special responsibility. All textbooks should be free of gender bias and strive for inclusive curricula. Textbooks are needed that discuss sex equity and provide teaching strategies for creating a classroom environment free of sex bias (Sadker et al., 1987). Introductory course texts should examine sexism and sexual harassment from legal, ethical, psychological, and educational perspectives. Students should learn to select appropriate textbooks for the classes they will offer in K–16 institutions.

Counselors

Counselor education should include a focus on proactive and reactive measures regarding sexual harassment. Counselors should be prepared in the area of sexual harassment to conduct educational workshops, crisis intervention, conflict resolution, intake procedures, and support groups for those who have been harassed. A counselor sometimes may be asked to serve as a consultant or grievance board member, or to educate the community about sexual harassment. In addition to psychosocial issues, counselors should be aware of sexual harassment policies, grievance procedures, and educational programs available on this issue.

Counselors in work, community, and school settings are likely to encounter clients who have been sexually harassed. For example, consider the following case of sexual abuse of a student reported by a guidance counselor: "The police said the student . . . was often truant and was referred to a guidance counselor. During one of their meetings, the student said one of the reasons she did not want to come to school was because she was being sexually abused" (Sullivan, 1995, p. B8).

Students training to be counselors should be knowledgeable about the psychodynamics of sexual harassment and the likely impact of the experience. They should be prepared to work with individuals experiencing sexual harassment, both the harassed and the harasser. Counselors must learn how to avoid "blaming the victim" and yet assist the person who has been harassed, the survivor, to examine the circumstances of the harassment, including which of their own judgments and actions advertently or inadvertently may have contributed to the situation. It is only after a careful understanding of this behavior, and the chance to examine alternatives, that the person will be truly empowered to get beyond and learn from the experience.

Exploration of the responsibility of the person harassed was more difficult some years ago. Women's movement advocates courageously asserted the rights of the person who had experienced sexual harassment. In their advocacy role they considered any exploration of the harassed's role as part of the age-old societal pattern of blaming the victim. Times have changed. It is now possible and important to assist, without blaming, the person who has been harassed in exploring all aspects of the experience, including the issue of responsibility. (I recall a class I was teaching at Yale in the late 1970s in which an attempt was made to discuss the experience of someone who had been raped. Given the prevailing attitude that was shared by students in the class, it was impossible to consider fully the experience of the person raped or harassed. As a reflection of the times, 15 years later in a similar discussion, students at Teachers College, Columbia University, were open to considering these aspects.)

A psychologist from a college counseling center reports a session with a female undergraduate who indicates that she has been raped. The undergraduate describes getting drunk, going to a male student's room at 3 a.m., and willingly participating in sexual play for several hours before having sexual intercourse "somewhat against her will." The counselor asks, "Where were you?" The counselor and client proceed to a consideration of the circumstances and issues of responsibility. This consideration is crucial to the client's growth.

Clients who have been sexually harassed, especially by people they know, have particular difficulty with the issue of trust that is so important to the counseling relationship. For example, Sandberg and colleagues (1987) point out, "the victim's degree of self blame is often heightened because the rapist was an acquaintance" (p. 308). Counselor preparation should prepare students to respond to these complicated issues.

The counselor–client relationship may itself be misinterpreted or lead to actual instances of sexual harassment. The greatest number of cases leading to loss of license for psychologists is sexual misconduct (American Psychological Association Ethics Committee, 1994). According to self-reports and in violation of the code of ethics, 1 to 12.1% of male and .4 to 3% of female psychologists have had sexual relationships with clients (Pope, 1993). Some additional examples of sexual harassment that may occur during the counseling process include (1) a counseling intern who is propositioned by an undergraduate client at a field placement, and (2) a psychologist who engages in a sexual relationship with a client. Students preparing to be counselors should be prepared to respond to sexual harassment whether on campus, during an off-campus internship, or in a postgraduation work setting. Counselor educators and practitioners may need in-service training in order to ensure their understanding of the issue of sexual harassment.

Administrators

The preparation of school administrators should include discussions of how to lead a school that is free of sexual harassment. School personnel should be prepared to address sexism and sexual harassment in the classroom (Sadker et al., 1987). Training should cover legal, ethical, and psychological issues related to sexual harassment. Prospective administrators should be taught case law; effective investigative mechanisms; requirements for reporting criminal acts, including sexual assault; mediation techniques; and assessment of the effectiveness of school policies and procedures (Klein & Wilber, 1986). These administrators should be prepared to create the school climate and establish an environment that takes the prevention of sexual harassment seriously. They should, with the involvement of the community, develop strong sexual harassment policies and procedures. School administrators should support teachers, counselors, and students in developing educational programs to respond to and to prevent sexual harassment.

Working with Other Institutions*

Schools of education may help to eliminate sexual harassment through work with their own universities and with off-campus field placements. They may encourage the development of effective sexual harassment policies and procedures, assist in the education and sensitization of the larger campus community by offering courses and workshops on sexual harassment open to the whole campus, act as a resource for information about sexual harassment, and call attention to the university's responsibility for preventing sexual harassment in off-campus programs and activities. In particular, teacher preparation programs can highlight the responsibility schools have to off-campus programs and develop constructive educational responses that will be applicable to other areas that require students to study and participate off campus.

Because the school of education and the field placement sites are both responsible for preventing sexual harassment, there is a need for cooperation. Some suggestions for collaboration are

- Screen and educate personnel, student teachers, cooperating teachers, and supervisors about sexual harassment
- Set up a joint committee to review the K–12 setting and the school of education for sexual harassment policy, practices, and nonhostile climate (This also may provide ways to educate the community regarding gender equity and sexual harassment.)
- Conduct workshops about sexual harassment for teacher preparation program personnel from cooperating institutions
- Review sexual harassment policy and grievance procedures
- Develop an understanding of the communication lines to be followed if a sexual harassment complaint involves persons from both institutions (This would be particularly demanding in schools of education that place students in many different field sites. Supervisors would require training and support to establish these arrangements.)
- Train personnel from both sites to understand sexual harassment, educate communities about sexual harassment, and receive complaints
- Plan educational programs at both institutions to deal with sexual harassment
- Transform curricula to include a consideration of sexual harassment and its underlying issues

---

*Portions of this information have been published as Brandenburg (1995).

- Work with parents and community groups
- Educate for change

Schools of education and K–12 schools often work together in partnerships and collaborations. A relationship between these institutions requires sensitivity and trust. A joint consideration of the issue of sexual harassment might be challenging but would likely deepen the connections and redound in great benefit to both institutions.

MIDDLE AND HIGH SCHOOL LEVELS

The incidence of sexual harassment is particularly high in grades 7 through 12. Educators need to respond to incidents of sexual harassment, develop curricula addressing gender, identify resources, and involve the broader school community (including parents) in combating sexual harassment. Workshops and presentations on sexual harassment for educators, students, and parents at the middle and high school levels can include discussions of acceptable adolescent behaviors and the development of personal and sexual identity.

A comprehensive study by the American Association of University Women (AAUW, 1992) underscores how sexism in school curricula has persisted in our schools, especially at the secondary level. Analysis of U.S. history textbooks reveals that material on women is scarce and that women's lives are trivialized, distorted, or omitted altogether. Of the 10 books used most frequently in high school English, only one was written by a woman (AAUW, 1992). History and English curricula for elementary and secondary school students can be transformed to include the efforts, lives, and writings of women. The curricula in other subjects, including physics and chemistry, also can be better linked to more representative examples that include the experiences of women. Teachers should be encouraged and assisted in selecting texts and curricular materials with gender equity in mind. The development of inclusive curricula that promote equity is likely to reduce the environment that supports sexual harassment.

Students may be assisted in setting up their own activities or groups to support each other and to learn about what can be done. A number of such programs are described by Henneberger (1994). Students at Fair Lawn High School in New Jersey established a women's issues club to help them deal with the barrage of sexual put-downs they received from their male counterparts. Other efforts undertaken at high schools across the country include lobbying to obtain space for a women's library and for adequate bathroom facilities, obtaining better financing and treatment for sports, and publishing a resource guide, "Young Women: Our Rights and Our Resources." In addition, FUTURE (Females Unifying Teens to Undertake Responsible Education), a group in San Leandro, California, "has trained young men to talk to middle-school boys about date rape" (Henneberger, 1994, p. B2).

The approach of Higginson (1993), a junior high school teacher on Long Island, New York, suggests how the finest examples of educational practice can be brought to bear on the issue of sexual harassment. Higginson's eighth-grade students knew the term *sexual harassment* but had some typically adolescent concepts of it.

"Sexual harassment! He's sexually harassing me!"
"That's not harassment! I was only joking!"
"You can't get in trouble for that!"
"Girls love it; they just don't want to admit it!"
"Girls don't like getting their butts grabbed, you moron!"
"Guys can't get harassed unless they have an erection!"

Higginson (1993) revamped her social studies curriculum with the help of various school staff members.

- The students worked in small groups to develop a sexual harassment policy.
- The school administrators attended a presentation to hear the students' recommendations and took notes.
- The students' definition of sexual harassment had become clearer and had been expanded to include jokes, gestures, and taunting.
- They recognized the need for compassion and support.
- They recognized the role of education in preventing problems.
- They urged warnings, written apologies, guidance, and lectures from the dean, among other strategies for handling cases of sexual harassment.
- The assistant superintendent at the school established a task force to create a district-wide sexual harassment policy.

According to Higginson (1993):

The solution to a potentially explosive problem turned out to be a validation of current educational philosophy: interdisciplinary team teaching, cooperative learning, student empowerment, shared decision-making. The whole experience culminated in a moment in which

teachers, administrators, and students were all learning from one another. . . . And, throughout the entire time, not one phone call had
come in objecting to the sensitive discussions or the time "lost" from
the standard curriculum. (pp. 95–96)

EARLY AND ELEMENTARY SCHOOL LEVELS

Unfortunately, sex discrimination and sexual harassment start as
features of American education even during the earliest years (AAUW,
1992; Pomerleau et al., 1990; Sadker et al., 1987). Gender bias estab-
lishes the norms and attitudes that lead people to believe that sexual
harassment is acceptable and permit educators to ignore harassing behaviors. Implicit in the goal of eliminating sexual harassment in education, is the elimination of sexism in early education through nonsexist
curricula and teaching practices. Workshops and presentations for preschool and elementary school teachers, day-care workers, parents, and
young children should consider sexual harassment in the broader context of gender bias and sexism, which are the precursors of sexual harassment.

Teachers must become aware of their perceptions and attitudes toward the behaviors of girls and boys. Teachers will need to monitor
their own language and behavior for biases, many of which are subtle
and deep-rooted. Teachers can suggest ways to eliminate bias from early
education and can point out behaviors currently reinforced in young
boys and girls that may contribute to sexual harassment. Appropriate
and inappropriate behaviors can be encouraged even for the youngest
students. Teachers of young children should assign activities to their
students that are gender neutral and should encourage both girls and
boys to engage in active as well as quiet play. Teachers can support sex
equity in their classrooms by selecting nonbiased curricular materials
that depict both sexes as engaging in a full range of human experience
and represent men and women in a nonstereotypic manner. Teachers of
young children can show them how to analyze their picture books,
nursery rhymes, and readers for gender stereotyping (Froschl & Sprung,
1988).

In Chapter 5, the example of Rose, the 3-year-old whose mother
was told to dress her in pants and teach her to say no, exemplifies
broad social patterns that are carried into the classroom. Even as Rose's
teacher may have been attempting to support Rose and to end behavior
that was a precursor to sexual harassment, she probably was unaware
of her own gender bias. The message the teacher conveyed, perhaps

unwittingly, was that the girl is responsible for rectifying the problem situation by modifying her own behavior, whereas the boy is not responsible and need not change.

There are many ways to avoid similar scenarios, most of which could be learned in a sexual harassment workshop and applied in the classroom as incidents occur. The teacher would monitor the behavior of her students differently. Rather then offering strategies only to Rose (and her mother), the teacher also would assist the boys (and their parents) to understand their responsibilities and would help all students to learn acceptable behavior. The teacher might arrange a discussion or workshop on sexual harassment for parents and would collaborate in learning how to check children's inappropriate behavior.

CONSIDERATIONS FOR PARENT EDUCATION

Education to stop sexual harassment must extend to the broader community, including parents. Efforts to prevent sexual harassment will be more effective when they are mutually reinforced at school and at home. For this reason, educators, particularly at the elementary and secondary levels, may wish to collaborate with the parents of their students. We need to educate parents about sexual harassment and to let them know that the school is concerned about this important issue. We should enlist parents in what can be done and utilize those parents with relevant expertise as resources in addressing this issue.

Parents can be invited to participate in workshops, discussion groups, and other projects at the school. Educational programs for parents should define sexual harassment, communicate the school's sexual harassment policy and procedures, and explicate the strategies for handling sexual harassment. Educational presentations for parents also can discuss sex education, sex equity, and sexism as factors underlying sexual harassment. Consideration may be given to the related issue of unequal distribution of power in society and how these issues are reflected in the school and the home.

The school could assist parents in defining their own role in efforts to eliminate sexual harassment. School personnel can encourage parents to educate themselves about sexual harassment, sexism, and gender-fair child-rearing practices. Parents should be provided with relevant information and resources.

Parent education regarding sexual harassment can be built on some very promising programs dealing with sex education that are already available. These programs typically include information on sexual development, improving communication skills, and supporting youngsters in resisting social and peer pressure. A national program, Postponing Sexual Involvement, prepares parents to help their teens postpone sexual involvement through resisting social and peer pressures (Howard & McCabe, 1990). The Center for Family Life Education (sponsored by Planned Parenthood of Greater New Jersey) offers programs for parents that involve (1) talking with preschoolers and adolescents, (2) sexual development, and (3) puberty education and enhancing self-esteem. The program, There's No Place Like Home . . . for Sex Education, includes: (1) sharing family values, (2) providing accurate information, (3) building effective decisions, and (4) counteracting negative and exploitive sexual messages in the media (Widoff, 1989). With the experience of these programs and an awareness of sexual harassment, parents can help their youngsters to become more assertive and to avoid or deal with situations where sexual harassment may occur.

CONCLUSION

Educational strategies are needed for schools at all levels to address and prevent sexual harassment. Institutions of higher education have instituted sexual harassment policies and grievance procedures, but many request assistance in developing educational strategies. Strategies already utilized in some institutions include workshops for incoming students and staff, peer counseling, and to a far lesser extent the inclusion of the issue of sexual harassment in the curricula. Schools of education have a special responsibility to provide a model environment free of sexual harassment, to prepare educational leaders, and to work with other institutions to eliminate sexual harassment. Suggestions are made for revising the curricula and for including the issue of sexual harassment in the preparation of teachers, counselors, administrators, and other professionals.

Education about sexual harassment and its underlying causes is needed particularly in preschool through high school. Students should learn about acceptable behavior and respect for others, and experience nonsexist curricula and teaching practices. Educational efforts include workshops, curricular revision, student activities, and the development and selection of textbooks free of gender bias. Educational efforts to address sexual harassment may be most effective when they involve parents. It is important that both school and home reinforce what is learned. This chapter provides suggestions and examples of educational strategies for elementary through postsecondary schools and for parent education. Resources to support these strategies are found in Appendix B.

Frequently Asked Questions About Sexual Harassment and Schools

Sexual harassment is an important, complicated, and widespread problem in our society and in our schools. It is defined as unwanted sexual attention that would be offensive to a reasonable person and that negatively affects the work or school environment. Sexual harassment involves a wide range of behavior from verbal innuendo and subtle suggestions to overt demands and sexual abuse. Sexual harassment is a form of sex discrimination that presents an insidious barrier to equal educational opportunity for all. Besides being unethical, sexual harassment is illegal. Schools are required to prohibit sexual harassment on campus and in their off-campus programs and activities.

The main hope for addressing and preventing sexual harassment is education. A comprehensive educational effort requires further research on the underlying causes of sexual harassment and on the development, utilization, and effectiveness of policies, procedures, and educational interventions. The best practices must be identified and new ones should be developed and evaluated. However, schools do not have the luxury to wait and are legally mandated to end sexual harassment now. What is needed is a multidimensional approach that includes establishing effective sexual harassment policies and grievance procedures, and creating educational interventions and systemic institutional change.

Over the past 19 years, in the course of my work on sexual harassment, I have been asked a variety of questions by educators, administrators, teachers, counselors, trustees, parents, and students. The following section includes 10 of the most frequently asked questions and my responses, informed by the many who have shared their experiences with me. These responses may serve to highlight some of the central issues of this book.

1. How Do I Get My School to Take the Issue of Sexual Harassment Seriously?

School leadership may still need to be educated about the issue of sexual harassment. A combination of data and moral suasion should convince the school administration that sexual harassment is a serious issue with potentially devastating consequences. The administration may need to be reminded that sexual harassment is illegal (see Chapter 2). Schools that fail to prohibit sexual harassment and to provide grievance procedures increase their liability and the prospect of lawsuits and damages. Schools that continue to ignore the issue of sexual harassment risk a great deal financially, reputationally, and educationally.

2. Do Institutions Need a Separate Grievance Procedure for Sexual Harassment Complaints?

While academic institutions are required by Title IX to have a grievance procedure for sexual harassment complaints, this need not be a separate procedure. Complaints of sexual harassment may be heard under a general grievance procedure. However, a separate sexual harassment grievance procedure that serves to highlight the importance of the issue may be preferable, depending on the context, size, situation, reputation, and history of sexual harassment at the institution (see Chapter 4). A large number of postsecondary institutions have separate sexual harassment grievance procedures.

3. Where Is the Line Between Acceptable Social Interaction (Flirting) and Sexual Harassment?

The critical element in sexual harassment is unwanted sexual attention. Some instances of sexual harassment, including quid pro quo harassment, appear to be clear-cut. However, sexual harassment has a subjective component, and behavior that may be welcome and experienced as flirting by one person may be frightening and harassing to someone else. The courts are struggling to find a "reasonable person" or "reasonable woman" standard in defining sexual harassment. Until this behavior is clarified, and society develops a shared understanding of what constitutes sexual harassment, a certain amount of ambiguity and self-consciousness in personal interactions is to be expected (see Chapter 1).

The distinction between acceptable interaction and sexual harassment may be particularly unclear among peers or persons of similar status (faculty colleagues, students, etc.). The line between these behaviors may be more clear when two persons of unequal authority or status are involved. Many suggest that persons in positions of authority, including teachers, advisors, coaches, and supervisors, should refrain from any social and personal relationship with those they supervise (see

Chapter 4 and Appendix A). Some academic institutions have explicit policies that prohibit personal relationships between staff and those they supervise or teach (see Appendix A). Other institutions rely on the judgment of those involved.

4. What Can a School Representative Do If a Student Reports a Situation of Sexual Harassment but Is Not Willing to Make a Complaint and Requests That Nothing Be Done?

In this instance the school representative (faculty, administrator, grievance officer) may be torn between the institution's responsibility to prevent sexual harassment, provide a nonhostile environment, and respond promptly to instances of sexual harassment, on the one hand, and the institution's commitment to honor confidentiality and the wishes of the individual reporting the alleged sexual harassment, on the other. Failure to honor confidentiality may betray a trust and decrease the likelihood that others will come forward with sexual harassment complaints.

The school representative should explore with the student the circumstances of the incident and the available avenues of recourse. The student may prefer to resolve matters on her or his own or with the assistance of the school grievance officer. The student may request a limited identification complaint, which enables the grievance officer to proceed by speaking to the person named in the complaint without describing the specific incident of alleged sexual harassment or identifying the student complaining (see Chapter 4). If such direct approaches are not acceptable, the grievance officer may utilize less direct alternatives that do not betray confidentiality. For example, it is possible that a "third party" to the incident may be encouraged to come forward to register a complaint. In addition, the grievance officer may initiate a generic effort to educate and sensitize about sexual harassment that is focused on a portion of the community that includes the person named.

5. What Are the Risks or Possible Costs to the Person Bringing a Complaint of Sexual Harassment?

Sexual harassment is often a difficult matter to prove. There is a cost for not taking action when one is being sexually harassed. However, the process of bringing a complaint may also take a toll on one's personal and academic life. It is important that a person confronting the decision of whether to make a formal complaint of sexual harassment have a realistic understanding of what is involved. The grievance officer should assist the person in exploring the options and the possible consequences of making a complaint (without either encouraging or discouraging this action). A person bringing a complaint may experience a sense of relief and satisfaction at taking an action. The complainant sometimes may (even without a formal procedure) be able to improve her or his work or school situation by changing instructors, housing, and so on. In other circumstances, direct relief may not be readily available (for example, the case of a graduate student who may have a complaint against the only member of the faculty who specializes in the field she wishes to pursue). Unfortunately, the person complaining also may encounter a grievance process that is long and time-consuming, be subject to close personal scrutiny, and experience a lack of support and even hostility from other members of the academic community (see Chapter 4).

6. What Is the Institutional Responsibility for an Incident of Sexual Harassment That Occurs While a Student Is Participating in an Off-Campus Activity or Program?

This question is of particular interest to professional schools, those with school-to-work programs, and others that have programs of study that require students to work in settings off campus. Schools are legally responsible for prohibiting sexual harassment in programs and activities off campus as well as on campus. It is important that schools develop sexual harassment policies and procedures that include off-campus settings. Schools should work with off-campus settings to educate personnel regarding the prevention of sexual harassment, and should take prompt action in the event of an instance of sexual harassment off campus (see Chapters 2, 4, and 6).

7. Are Matters of Sexual Assault, Sexual Abuse, and Rape Forms of Sexual Harassment? How Should They Be Handled by the School?

Sexual assault, sexual abuse, and rape are severe forms of sexual harassment that are included under Title IX and are felonies that require special legal consideration. All states require the reporting of instances of child sexual abuse (see Chapter 1).

A person who has been raped or sexually assaulted may go directly to the police. However, students often prefer internal school grievance procedures to outside adjudication. School procedures may be perceived as more sensitive than the courts and as having a more flexible standard of proof. Sometimes both internal and external procedures are sought or required. The school must determine when to investigate and how to respond to the incident vis-à-vis the court process. Schools differ in the type of procedures they have for handling these matters. Complaints sometimes are heard under sexual harassment grievance procedures and sometimes under disciplinary procedures for violations of the behavioral code (see Chapter 4).

8. Is Harassment of People Due to Their Sexual Orientation a Form of Sexual Harassment?

Sexual harassment sometimes occurs between same-sex persons or people who are homosexual. Harassment based on sexual orientation, referred to as "gay bashing," includes a broad range of behaviors, which may or may not be sexual harassment (see Chapter 1). Strictly speaking, only those instances of harassment based on sexual orientation that involve unwanted sexual attention are considered sexual harassment. Nonetheless, some schools receive all complaints of harassment based on sexual orientation under their sexual harassment grievance procedures (see Chapter 4).

9. How Can a School Determine Whether It Is Being Effective in Preventing Sexual Harassment and a Hostile Environment?

It is difficult to know whether an institution is being effective in prohibiting sexual harassment. If a school has strong sexual harassment policies and grievance procedures and few sexual harassment complaints, it might mean either that these efforts are effective or that people are unaware or distrustful of the procedures. Schools must do all they can on an ongoing basis to educate the community about sexual harassment. Definitions must be clear and educational interventions developed to enlighten the community. Surveys and focus groups can be used to evaluate sexual harassment policies, procedures, and educational strategies (see Chapters 4, 5, and 6).

10. How Can We Prohibit Sexual Harassment Without Infringing on People's Privacy and Freedom?

Educational institutions are and should be bastions of freedom of speech, individual rights, and academic freedom. An atmosphere that limits these freedoms is surely antithetical to learning. The tolerance of sexual harassment as well as the curtailment of academic freedom and freedom of speech may deprive members of the community of their rightful education. The tensions among these sometimes competing freedoms can be resolved through education and the development of sensitive and effective policies and grievance procedures (see Chapter 4). Representatives of all viewpoints should be invited to debate the issues and should be included in the development of sexual harassment polices and grievance procedures. These policies and procedures must avoid vague definitions and balance the rights of the individual with the interests of the community.

There is much that schools can and must do to address and prevent sexual harassment. A sustained effort is required which includes educational programs and systematic institutional change, as well as effective sexual harassment policies and grievance procedures. This effort is critical as it represents our best hope to ensure equal educational opportunity and to guarantee humane and respectful treatment for all.

Current State, Local, and Institutional Policies and Grievance Procedures on Sexual Harassment

Sexual harassment policies and grievance procedures relevant to educational institutions have been developed at the federal, state, local, and institutional level. The key federal regulations that govern institutional policies and procedures on sexual harassment, Title VII of the Civil Rights Act of 1964 and Title IX of the Education Amendments of 1972, are discussed in Chapters 1 and 2. Aspects of creating sexual harassment policies and procedures are described in Chapter 4. For further information and assistance regarding these regulations, and for brief descriptions of some additional laws with relevance to sexual harassment and schools, see Appendix C.

This appendix includes excerpts and descriptive summaries of policies and grievance procedures at state, local, and individual school levels. Selections were made to illustrate a range of examples and should be evaluated by the reader. The New Haven Public School procedure, a comprehensive procedure, is included almost in its entirety. Educators who wish to adapt any of the following policies and procedures to their own institutions should ensure that their efforts are in compliance with federal, state, and local legal requirements. All institutions should seek legal counsel when developing a sexual harassment policy or grievance procedure. The examples include

- State level: California, Massachusetts, Minnesota, New Jersey, New York
- Local level: New York City Board of Education; New Haven Public Schools; Ridgewood, New Jersey, Public Schools

- Individual school level:
  K–12: Oregon Episcopal School, Minuteman Science–Technology High School, The Hotchkiss School
  Postsecondary: Yale University, State University of New York at Albany, University of Iowa, Teachers College, Columbia University

STATE LEVEL

A number of states have taken steps to address sexual harassment within their schools. This section reviews policies available in five states—California, Massachusetts, Minnesota, New Jersey, and New York.

California

California State Department of Education
Legal Office, 721 Capitol Mall, Room 552
P.O. Box 944272
Sacramento, CA 94244-2720
Telephone: (916) 657-2453
Fax: (916) 657-3844

California Department of Health Services—Office of Family Planning
P.O. Box 942732
Sacramento, CA 94234-7320
Telephone: (916) 654-0357
Fax: (916) 657-1608

The policy on sexual harassment issued by the California State Department of Education prohibits sexual harassment as a form of sexual discrimination, provides notification of available remedies, and mandates that all educational institutions publicize and disseminate their written policies. The policy states, in part:

(b) Each educational institution in the State of California shall have a written policy on sexual harassment. . . .
(c) The educational institution's written policy on sexual harassment shall include information on where to obtain the specific rules and procedures for reporting charges of sexual harassment and for pursuing available remedies.
. . .

(e) A copy of the educational institution's written policy on sexual harassment, as it pertains to students, shall be provided as part of any orientation program conducted for new students at the beginning of each quarter, semester, or summer session, as applicable.

(f) A copy of the educational institution's written policy on sexual harassment shall be provided for each faculty member, all members of the administrative staff, and all members of the support staff at the beginning of the first quarter or semester of the school year, or at the time that there is a new employee hired. (California State Department of Education, 1992, § 212.6: Educational institutions; written policy on sexual harassment)

The statewide effort to educate teenagers to postpone sexual involvement, ENABL, undertaken by the California State Department of Health Services, is reviewed in Appendix B.

Massachusetts

Massachusetts Department of Education
Instruction and Curriculum Services
350 Main Street
Malden, MA 02148-5023
Telephone: (617) 388-3300

The policy of the State of Massachusetts states:

Whereas, sexual harassment undermines the integrity of the workplace and the personal dignity of the individual; and

Whereas, sexual harassment may involve a person of either sex against a person of the same or opposite sex; and

Whereas, it is the policy of the Commonwealth to prevent and eliminate sexual harassment in state employment, to ensure that state employees are permitted to work in an atmosphere free from sexual harassment;

. . .

The Executive Office of Administration and Finance shall establish procedures for the handling of grievances pertaining to sexual harassment in state employment in all state agencies under all Executive Offices, the Board of Regents of Higher Education and the Board of Education. Said grievance procedures shall be posted by every state agency, appointing authority, board, commission, or office subject to this order. (Commonwealth of Massachusetts, 1981)

See Appendix B for materials developed by Massachusetts.

Minnesota

Office of the Attorney General, Minnesota
102 State Capitol
St. Paul, MN 55155
Telephone: (612) 296-6196
                 (800) 657-3787 (TDD or voice)
Fax: (612) 297-4193

The State of Minnesota, which has some of the most clearly defined laws in this area, requires that all public junior and senior high schools have a written policy regarding sexual harassment, and that all postsecondary institutions participating in state financial aid programs provide each student with written policies regarding sexual harassment and sexual violence. With reference to higher education, the Minnesota law states:

> Each campus plan shall address at least the following components:
> 1) security such as type and level of security systems on campus, including physical plant, escort services, and other human resources; and
> 2) training such as programs or other efforts to provide mandatory training to faculty, staff and students regarding campus policies and procedures relating to incidents of violence and sexual harassment and the extent and causes of violence. (Higher Education Coordinating Board and Office of the Attorney General, 1993, Appendix A)

The Minnesota Human Rights Act prohibits sexual harassment as a form of sex discrimination, and the Minnesota Human Rights Department has the authority to investigate formal complaints of sexual harassment. The Office of the Attorney General of the State of Minnesota makes available a range of documents and resource materials addressing issues on sexual harassment, including policy making and training faculty and students about sexual harassment policies and procedures for handling incidents of sexual harassment. See Appendix B for materials developed by Minnesota.

New Jersey

New Jersey Department of Education
Bureau of Student Behavior and Development

Division of General Academic Education
225 West State Street
Trenton, NJ 08625

The New Jersey Administrative Code Regulations Governing School Desegregation address equal educational opportunity. The regulations prohibit discrimination, including that on the basis of sex, but do not specifically mention sexual harassment. The following section has an indirect bearing on sexual harassment:

> All New Jersey public school districts shall comply with all State and Federal laws related to equal employment, including . . . Title VII . . . and Title IX. (New Jersey Department of Education, 1977, 6: 4-1.6, Employment/Contract Practices)

Family Life Education Programs: In 1980, New Jersey mandated family life education for grades K–12. According to the New Jersey Administrative Code (Title 6, Education, Subchapter 7, Family Life Education Programs):

> Family life education program means instruction to develop an understanding of the . . . mental, emotional, social, . . . and psychological aspects of interpersonal relationships; the . . . psychological and cultural foundations of human development, sexuality, and reproduction, at various stages of growth. (Sprung, 1992, p. 2)

The mandate requires all K–12 school districts to have a family life education program at the elementary and secondary levels covering the areas of interpersonal relationships; foundations of human growth and development; responsible personal behavior; and establishment of strong family life. Following New Jersey, more than 20 other states have adopted family life or sex education mandates. Such initiatives offer an opportunity to address gender bias in educational practice and to include education about sexual harassment.

New York State

New York State Education Department
Room 667, Education Building Annex
Albany, NY 12234
Telephone: (518) 474-5923

The New York State Education Department has adopted a sexual harassment policy for its employees in accordance with Title VII of the Civil Rights Act of 1964 and the New York State Human Rights Law. Sexual harassment is included as a category within the general antidiscrimination policies.

> Every State Education Department employee is entitled to a working environment free from sexual harassment. It has no place in the workplace. Ignoring the problem is tolerating the problem, and the State is determined that harassment of any sort will not be tolerated. Sexual harassment is considered to be a form of misconduct, and sanctions will be enforced against supervisory and managerial personnel who knowingly allow such behavior to exist in the workplace as well as against those persons guilty of such misbehavior. (University of the State of New York, 1993, p. 47)

See Appendix B section for materials developed by New York.

LOCAL LEVEL

New York City

New York City Board of Education—Office of Equal Opportunity
110 Livingston Street
Brooklyn, NY 11201
Telephone: (718) 935-3602
Fax: (718) 935-3775

Procedure for Complaints of Alleged Discrimination by Students, Parents of Students, and Employees, Including Complaints of Sexual Harassment Policy Issued: July 1988

New York City Public Schools are covered by Regulation A-830, *Procedure for Complaints of Alleged Discrimination by Students, Parents of Students, and Employees, Including Complaints of Sexual Harassment Policy*, issued by the Chancellor, providing for an internal review process for handling discrimination complaints, including sexual harassment, and for the maintenance of an environment free of sexual harassment. These provisions are in accordance with federal and state laws.

Regulation A-830 outlines, in detail, procedures for handling complaints (including anonymous complaints) and designates the Local Equal Opportunity Coordinator (LEOC) as the official authorized to handle them. LEOCs can be appointed at the district and the high school levels. It is their role to handle complaints and to provide accessible information on equal educational and employment opportunities. Regulation A-830 also includes a provision for interim relief.

Policy (excerpts)

(1) It is the policy of the Board of Education to provide equal educational and employment opportunities without regard to race, color, creed, national origin, age, marital status, handicapping condition, sexual orientation, or sex and to maintain an environment free of sexual harassment. . . .

(2) The above laws also prohibit retaliation against any individuals for utilizing the following procedures or filing charges with one of the governmental civil rights agencies.

(3) Federal and state law require the Board of Education to develop and maintain a school/office environment free of discrimination, sexual harassment, and intimidation. In order to achieve this goal, the full cooperation of every staff member is expected. Specifically, staff members are expected to be exemplary role models in the schools and offices which they serve. Employees found to be in violation of this policy and these laws may be subject to administrative and legal sanctions. (City School District of the City of New York, 1988, p. 2)

Procedures (description)

Procedures for complaints of alleged discrimination by students, parents of students, and employees, including complaints of sexual harassment:

1) Three types of complaints and accompanying procedures.
   Conciliation of Complaints
   Formal Review of Complaints
   Anonymous Complaints
2) Complaints are handled by the LEOC assigned to each community school district, high school, and division office. A complaint also may be filed with the Office of Equal Opportunity (OEO).

Procedures for complaints alleging sexual harassment
  A. All complaints alleging sexual harassment must be filed with
      the LEOC or OEO within thirty (30) days of the alleged act. See
      procedures for conciliation and formal review.
  B. A complaint alleging sexual harassment may be requested to be
      handled exclusively by OEO. (City School District of the City
      of New York, 1988, p. 11)
3) Interim Relief
4) Process of Appeal

See Appendix B for materials developed by New York City Board of
Education.

New Haven, CT

New Haven Public Schools
Administrative Office
Gateway Center
54 Meadow Street
New Haven, CT 06519
Telephone: (203) 946-8801

Sexual Harassment Policy and Procedure
Issued: April 1994

Employees and students of the New Haven Public School System
are protected under the provisions of Title VII of the Civil Rights Act of
1964, the Connecticut Fair Employment Practices Act, and/or Title IX
of the Education Amendments of 1972. The New Haven Board of Education has a very comprehensive and clear sexual harassment policy and
grievance procedure in effect for the New Haven Public Schools. All
employees, students, and parents are provided with copies of the sexual
harassment policy through individual distribution or publications, such
as employee and student handbooks. All administrators and supervisors
of the New Haven Public Schools receive training on the subject of
sexual harassment.

Policy (excerpts)

Sexual harassment is a form of sexual discrimination and is illegal
under both federal and state laws.
   Should sexual harassment be alleged, it is the policy of the New
Haven Board of Education that the allegation(s) shall be thoroughly

investigated, that there shall be no retaliation against the victim of the alleged harassment, and that the issue shall be expeditiously and appropriately addressed. (New Haven Board of Education, 1994, p. 1)

Procedure (excerpt)

The purpose of the following procedure is to ensure that the New Haven school district remains in compliance with State and federal laws regarding discrimination and sexual harassment. All proceedings shall be kept confidential to the extent consistent with the Board's obligations under law and its obligations to investigate. Any reprisals against a complaint or witness shall be viewed as a violation of the New Haven Public School Sexual Harassment Policy and subject to appropriate, independent disciplinary action, up to and including termination.

Informal Process

Prior to the filing of a formal sexual harassment complaint, an individual may seek resolution through an informal process. This avenue may be appropriate in situations where possible miscommunication has occurred, or where thoughtless, unintentional behavior has caused distress. Under the informal process, the individual who believes that she/he has been harassed should immediately inform the other party that the behavior is unwelcome, illegal, offensive, unprofessional, inappropriate, or in poor taste. Such communication may be oral or in writing should include a description of the offensive behavior and a request that such behavior cease. It is strongly recommended that, regardless of the manner employed to address the issue of harassment, the victim should keep detailed written notes on all incidents which the individual believes comprise sexual harassment. *This informal process is discretionary on the part of the individual who believes she/he has been harassed and is not a required part of the Board of Education's complaint Procedure which may be commenced as described below.*

Formal Process

Any employee or applicant for employment who wishes to register a complaint alleging discrimination or sexual harassment in the New Haven public school system may file such a complaint with her/his immediate supervisor, or the Director of Staff Placement, Evaluation and Development or the Executive Director of Pupil Personnel Services. Any student, parent or guardian who wishes to register a complaint alleging discrimination or sexual harassment in the New Haven public school system may file a complaint with the relevant principal, the Chief Executive Director, the Executive Director or the Superintendent of Schools. The Superintendent of Schools and the Chairperson of the Board will be notified immediately of all complaints and the Superintendent of Schools shall notify the Board of Education at its next regular meeting.

Upon the filing of a complaint, a thorough, objective and complete investigation of all allegations will be undertaken. The investigator(s) may consult with the Board's attorneys with the approval of the Chairperson of the Board. The investigation may involve all individuals reasonably believed to have relevant information, including the complainant, the individual accused in the complaint, witnesses and individuals who are alleged to have been the victims of similar conduct. The investigator shall make a written report with the results of the investigation and recommendations for the disposition of the matter to the Superintendent of Schools. Copies shall be provided to the complainant and the individual accused in the complaint. The Superintendent of Schools shall take action as she/he deems appropriate, which action may include a recommendation to the Board that an employee who has been determined to have committed sexual harassment be terminated from her/his employment. The Board shall act upon such a recommendation in executive session, subject to the rights of tenured certified employees to have a hearing before an impartial hearing panel or the right under the Connecticut Freedom of Information Act of a public employee to require such meeting to take place in public session.

At all times during the Complaint Procedure, the representatives of the New Haven public schools should be cognizant of and endeavor to protect the legal rights of all parties involved. Additionally, confidentiality shall be maintained to the extent consistent with the Board's obligations under law and its obligations to investigate.

This Complaint Procedure is not exclusive and complainants may have additional legal rights, including the right to file charges with the Connecticut Commission on Human Rights and Opportunities, the Equal Employment Opportunity Commission and/or United States Department of Education.

In response to incidents of sexual harassment, the Superintendent of Schools, in her/his discretion, may take any of the following actions:

• reprimand or warning;
• reassignment;
• transfer;
• suspension or recommendation of suspension to the Board;
• demotion or recommendation of demotion to the Board;
• expulsion (student) in accordance with applicable law; or
• recommendation to the Board of termination of employment;
• termination of contract

. . .

This procedure will be reviewed and updated periodically. Education and training sessions which define sexual harassment and explain this procedure will be offered to all supervisory employees as required by State law and shall be offered to other staff members and students as deemed advisable by the Board of Education . . . *No form of harassment will be tolerated in the New Haven public schools.* (New Haven Board of Education, 1994, pp. 2–5).

Ridgewood, NJ

Ridgewood Public Schools
Board of Education
49 Cottage Place
Ridgewood, NJ 07451
Telephone: (201) 670-2600

Educational Administration: Sexual Harassment
Issued: 1988
Amended: 1995

Policy and procedure (entire)

The Board of Education shall strive to maintain an instructional and working environment that is free from harassment of any kind. Administrators and supervisors will make it clear to all staff, pupils and vendors that harassment is prohibited. Sexual harassment shall be specifically addressed in the affirmative action inservice programs required by law for all staff.

Sexual harassment of staff or children interferes with the learning process and will not be tolerated in the Ridgewood Public Schools. Any child or staff member who has knowledge of or feels victimized by sexual harassment should immediately report his/her allegation to an equal educational opportunity officer or building principal. This policy statement will be distributed to all staff members.

Staff or pupils may file a formal grievance related to harassment on any of the grounds addressed in this policy. The equal educational opportunity officer(s) will receive all complaints and carry out a thorough investigation, and will protect the rights of both the person making the complaint and the alleged harasser. The equal educational opportunity officer(s) will make a determination or finding after conducting a thorough investigation.

Findings of discrimination or harassment will result in appropriate disciplinary action. (Ridgewood Board of Education, 1995, p. 1)

INDIVIDUAL SCHOOLS

K-12 Schools

Oregon Episcopal School
6300 SW Nicol Road
Portland, OR 97223

Abuse/Sexual Harassment
Issued: March 1992

The policy statement of the Oregon Episcopal School focuses on students, and distinguishes between child abuse and sexual harassment. It lists offices within the school where current laws and useful addresses and telephone numbers can be found, as well as school officials responsible for handling sexual harassment complaints. The statement also includes a commitment to providing regular inservice training to all employees and keeping them abreast of changes in the law.

Policy (description and excerpts)

> Oregon Episcopal School is committed to providing an environment free of harassment of any kind. Sexual harassment, harassment based on race, color, religion, or national origin are prohibited by law and contradictory to the school's policy. Any school employee who engages in harassment is subject to discipline, up to and including immediate termination. Any student who engages in harassment is subject to discipline, up to and including expulsion. Any employee or student who believes he/she is being harassed, or any employee who witnesses an incident of harassment, should contact their supervisor, division head, or headmaster. The matter will be promptly and thoroughly investigated. (Oregon Episcopal School, 1992, p. 2)

The policy covers the following:

1) Policy statement on child abuse and sexual harassment—Policy focuses on children as potential victims but also refers to adult to adult abuse and harassment.
2) Reporting child abuse—Any employee must report suspected abuse to his or her supervisor, division head, or the headmaster. In addition, the law requires any form of abuse to be reported to the local Children Services Division or other proper law enforcement agen-

cies. Anyone found guilty of any form of abuse will be terminated immediately.

3) Harassment—Policy statement covers all forms of harassment, including sexual harassment and harassment based on race, color, religion, or national origin. Proper action will be taken to discipline any employee or student found guilty of harassment. Victims of harassing behavior should contact their supervisor, division head, or the headmaster.

4) Inservice obligations of the institution—Training will be provided for all employees every 3 years to acquaint them with the school's abuse and harassment policy and procedures. All employees are required to attend. All new employees receive training as part of their orientation.

5) Curriculum obligation of the institution—The school will provide education to students on issues of harassment and abuse within the formal curriculum.

6) Discussion of some meanings of child abuse—Various types of abuse (physical abuse, physical neglect, psychological abuse, and sexual abuse) are defined.

7) Adult–adult and adult–adolescent sexual relationships
   A) Sexual relationships between adult employees and present students or recent graduates are always unacceptable. The policy discusses the influence of the power relationship.
   B) Forced sexual contact is defined and includes rape.
   C) Coerced sexual contact is defined and the power relationship is explained. The policy states that "a key to deciding if a relationship was coerced is whether one of the partners in the relationship felt pressured to participate even if they overtly agreed to it." (Oregon Episcopal School, 1992, p. 4)

8) Discussion of some meanings of sexual harassment
   A) Overt verbal harassment is defined and examples of unacceptable behavior are provided.
   B) Sexist teaching practices are prohibited, including gender stereotyping in the classroom. The policy states, "If a practice or comment would be racist in a racial context it is probably sexist in a gender context." (p. 5)

Procedures

1) *Complaints involving school employees*: Any report will be investigated and resolved, and a written report will be placed in a permanent confidential file for review by the headmaster or a designee.

2) *Complaints involving students*: Any report will be investigated and resolved, and a written report will be placed in a permanent confidential file for review by the headmaster or a designee.

Minuteman Science–Technology High School
758 Marrett Road
Lexington, MA 02173-7398
Telephone: (617) 861-6500

Guidelines for Recognizing and Dealing with Sexual Harassment
Issued: November 6, 1980
Revised: June 17, 1993

Minuteman Science–Technology High School has developed and revised its *Guidelines for Recognizing and Dealing with Sexual Harassment* for addressing sexual harassment as defined by Title VII. The document details steps the victim can take, including the components of a letter to the harasser, and the name and telephone extension of the contact person/official within the school.

Policies and procedures (excerpt)

Note: If a situation involving a charge of *teacher to student* sexual harassment is brought to the attention of any staff member, that staff member should notify [the Assistant Superintendent] *immediately* so that the situation can be resolved as confidentially and as quickly as possible in order to protect the rights of both parties.

1. By law, the victim defines sexual harassment. What one person may consider acceptable behavior may be viewed as sexual harassment by another person. Therefore, in order to protect the rights of both parties, it is important that the victim make it clear to the harasser that the behavior is bothering him or her. This can be done in ways described in items two and three below.

2. *Always take every report of sexual harassment seriously* and take some kind of action *immediately*, remember, "you can't argue with a feeling." Many times, situations involving student-to-student non-physical harassment can be quickly and quietly resolved if the harasser and the victim can be persuaded to sit down and talk things over in the presence of a third person.

3. If the victim does not agree to meet with the harasser, the victim should write the harasser a letter giving:
   (a) an exact description of the behavior, including when and where it occurred,

(b) a description of how the behavior made the victim feel—"embarrassed," "upset," "angry," etc.,

(c) a request that the behavior stop because it is sexual harassment and is against the law, and

(d) a promise that if the behavior stops, nothing further would be said, and no further action will be taken.

(e) a warning that showing the letter, and/or talking about to other students or engaging in any other retaliatory behavior will subject the harasser to disciplinary action.

The letter should be dated and signed by the victim, indicating that a copy of the letter has also been given to a school staff member. (This provides proof that the victim has made it clear to the harasser that the behavior is unacceptable and should be stopped.) The letter then should be hand delivered to the harasser by either the victim or the school staff member. In most instances, this will stop the harassment, if it doesn't, there is now a legal basis for taking further action.

Note: In the case of student-to-student harassment, the staff member to whom the student reports the harassment should sit down immediately with the student, help him/her draft the letter and make sure the letter is delivered.

4. In cases of sexual harassment requiring a formal investigation to determine whether or not the accusation is justified, it is important to:

(a) have a supportive faculty member of the same sex as the accuser present at all discussions with the accuser involving the case.

(b) keep the investigating group as small as possible to protect the rights of both parties and to prevent the investigation from becoming an inquisition.

Retaliation: Retaliation in any form against any person who has filed a complaint relating to sexual harassment is forbidden. If it occurs, it can be considered grounds for dismissal of school personnel and/or removal from the educational setting for a student.

Confidentiality: Reports of sexual harassment should be kept completely confidential, involving as few people as possible, with the goal of protecting both parties and stopping the behavior, rather than punishing anyone (unless the behavior was found to be so blatant and severe that the victim has suffered severe emotional and/or physical harm). (Minuteman Science–Technology High School, 1993, pp. 1–2).

The Hotchkiss School
P.O. Box 800
Lakeville, CT 06039-0800
Telephone: (860) 435-2591

Harassment Policy
Issued: March 1993

The Hotchkiss School explicitly prohibits employees from making any sexual advances toward students in light of the school's role as being *in loco parentis*.

Policy (excerpts)

Sexual harassment is a violation of laws against discrimination (Title VII of the Civil Rights Act of 1964). . . . Sexual harassment is unlawful even when the alleged conduct has caused an individual no economic harm or loss of other tangible job benefits.

Sexual harassment is not social or courting behavior. It is unwanted and is best seen as an assertion of power. . . .

It is important to remember that in faculty–student relationships in particular, the power imbalance, coupled with the student's relative inexperience, makes a strong sense of professional and institutional responsibility an imperative. Therefore, while unwelcome sexual advances, etc., are prohibited between employees at Hotchkiss, *all* sexual advances are prohibited with respect to students, even if a student is apparently accepting of them. The school acts *in loco parentis* for all students, and any hint of irresponsible behavior by faculty or staff is a breach of trust and creates a liability for the school. *Faculty and staff behavior with respect to students must be above suspicion.* (The Hotchkiss School, 1993, p. 1)

Procedures (excerpt)

Behavior perceived to constitute harassment should be brought to the attention of the student deans, the Provost, or the Dean of Faculty. Those found to be in violation of the above principle will be subject to appropriate action, including suspension or separation from the school. (The Hotchkiss School, 1993, p. 1)

Postsecondary Institutions

Yale College, Yale University
Dean of Student Affairs
PO Box 208241
New Haven, CT 06520-8241

Grievance Procedure for Complaints of Sexual Harassment
Issued: 1979
Revised: 1980, 1981, 1995

One of the first procedures for student complaints of sexual harassment, Yale College's procedure has been used as a model for other postsecondary schools. The seven-person grievance board that receives complaints from students at Yale College includes faculty, students, and administrators. The process includes informal resolution and formal complaints. The procedure has provisions for fully identified complaints with later identification, and complaints with limited identification. The process is confidential and symmetrical in protecting the rights of the person bringing the complaint and the person named. The board investigates and makes recommendations to the Dean. The Dean may take appropriate action or refer the complaint to appropriate disciplinary procedures. The 1995 revision of this procedure includes student to student complaints of sexual harassment. Previously, this type of complaint went directly to a student disciplinary committee.

Policy (excerpt)

> Sexual harassment is antithetical to academic values and to a work environment free from the fact or appearance of coercion. It is a violation of University policy and may result in disciplinary action. Sexual harassment consists of nonconsensual sexual advances, requests for sexual favors, or other verbal or physical conduct on or off campus, when: [EEOC guidelines]. Sexual harassment may be found in a single episode, as well as in persistent behavior. Conduct that occurs in the process of application for admission to a program or selection for employment is covered by this policy, as well as conduct directed toward University students, faculty or staff members. (Yale College, 1979–1995b, p. 10)

Procedure (excerpts)

> The board will emphasize mediation and conciliation and will rely on discreet inquiry, persuasion, confidentiality and trust in dealing with complaints that are brought for its consideration. When it cannot resolve a complaint to the satisfaction of those concerned, the Board will refer the matter in an advisory capacity with recommendations, to the Dean of Yale College. (Yale College, 1979–1995a, p. 2)

In many of these cases the board may simply act as an intermediary between the parties involved, or as an expediter in arranging meetings. In this mode of operation (in which the Board is acting less as an adjudicating body and more as a body to educate and heighten the awareness of the individuals involved), the Board will not act unilaterally but will seek the complaining student's consent in any action it takes. (p. 3)

The Board will limit its investigation to what may be necessary to resolve the complaint or to make a recommendation to the Dean. If it appears necessary for the Board to speak to any persons other than the persons involved in the complaint, it will do so only after informing the complaining person or persons and the person complained against. (p. 4)

The Dean's decision may be to take any actions as may be within his or her authority (e.g., issue any oral or written warning or reprimand to the individual against whom the complaint was lodged; permit a student to participate in an educational program or activity; institute academically appropriate procedures whereby a student's grade may be reviewed). If the remedy deemed appropriate by the Dean is beyond his or her authority, the Dean will recommend the initiation of such action (disciplinary or otherwise) in accordance with applicable University practices and procedures. (p. 5)

In general, an undergraduate may bring a complaint to the Board up to two years after the date of the incident. However, the Board is willing to discuss but may decide not to take formal action on a complaint about an incident of sexual harassment that happened more than two years after the date of the incident so long as it occurred any time while the complainant was an undergraduate. (p. 6)

If the complaint is not resolved by the Board or requires action which only the Dean can take, or the complaint needs further investigation or demands more serious sanctions or a formal disciplinary procedure, the complaint will be referred, with written recommendations by the board, to the Dean of Yale College. The Dean will review the Board's report, which will include statements of the student's complaint and the response by the person named in the complaint. The Dean will discuss the matter with both the person making the complaint and the person against whom the complaint is directed. It is recognized that referral of a particular case to the Dean may in itself represent a sanction. In cases where the Dean believes sanctions are appropriate, the Dean may issue a warning, a reprimand, or decide to recommend formal disciplinary action for the person named in the complaint.

In those cases in which, in the judgment of the Dean, formal disciplinary action against a faculty member or administrator is called for, the Dean will make such a recommendation to the Provost. (p. 7)

State University of New York at Albany
Administration 246
Albany, NY 12222

Policy on Sexual Harassment
Issued: January 1981
Revised: February 1991

The policy discusses faculty–student harassment, other forms of discrimination, and consensual relationships. It defines sexual harassment using the EEOC guidelines.

Policy (excerpt)

The University at Albany has long been dedicated to maintaining and fostering a fair, humane, and supportive environment for all of its students and staff. Sexual harassment in any of its forms has been and will continue to be considered a violation of policy and dealt with under the procedures that have been established. Any violation of these policies should be brought to the attention of the Affirmative Action office immediately. (State University of New York at Albany, 1991)

Procedures (description)

Customary incremental steps in the investigation of allegations of illegal discrimination include

1) Inquiries—Voicing one's concerns to the Affirmative Action (AA) office.
2) Complaints—Conferring with the Director or Associate Director of AA office to discuss the nature of the case and explore ways of resolution. The AA officer will contact accused harasser and indicate the voluntary nature of the procedure. A solution must be agreed upon within 10 working days.
3) Grievance—Submitting the grievance in writing on forms to AA office within stated time boundaries. If informal resolution fails, finding will be forwarded to the vice-president for a judgment.

University of Iowa
202 Jessup Hall
Iowa City, IA 52242

Policy on Sexual Harassment and Consensual Relationships
Issued: November 1986

Policy (excerpt and description)

(a) Sexual harassment is reprehensible and will not be tolerated by the University. It subverts the mission of the University and threatens the careers, educational experience, and well-being of students, faculty, and staff. Relationships involving sexual harassment or discrimination have no place within the University. In both obvious and subtle ways, the very possibility of sexual harassment is destructive to individual students, faculty, staff and the academic community as a whole. When, through fear of reprisal, a student, staff member, or faculty member submits or is pressured to submit to unwanted sexual attention, the University's ability to carry out its mission is undermined. (b) Sexual harassment is especially serious when it threatens relationships between teacher and student or supervisor and subordinate. In such situations, sexual harassment exploits unfairly the power inherent in a faculty member's or supervisor's position. Through grades, wage increases, recommendations for graduate study, promotion, and the like, a teacher or supervisor can have a decisive influence on a student's, staff member's, or faculty member's career at the University and beyond. (c) While sexual harassment most often takes place in situations of a power differential between the persons involved, the University also recognizes that sexual harassment may occur between persons of the same University status. The University will not tolerate behavior between or among members of the University community which creates an unacceptable working or educational environment. (University of Iowa, 1986, p. 1)

The policy covers the following:

1) Sexual harassment
   A) Rationale—University policy on sexual harassment condemns teacher–student as well as peer harassment.
   B) Prohibited acts—Sexual harassment is defined using the EEOC guidelines.
   C) Examples of sexual harassment—Behavioral descriptions are given, thereby indicating the broad nature of the problem.
   D) Isolated and inadvertent offenses—These are defined as offenses

in which the person doesn't know that the behavior is sexual harassment. The person must attend an educational program.
2) Consensual relationships
    A) Definition—Faculty is defined as all those who teach or have other instructional roles, including graduate students.
    B) Rationale—University policy on consensual relationships discusses the power dynamic between supervisor or teacher and student. The University views as unethical faculty members engaging in amorous relations with students in their classes or subject to their supervision, even when both parties appear to have consented to the relationship.
    C) Consensual relationships in the instructional context—Amorous relationships with students in their classes or under their supervision are prohibited.
    D) Consensual relationships outside the instructional context—These are not forbidden but are strongly advised against.

Procedures

1) *Informal complaint*: Complaint may be taken to any member of the University community (Director of Affirmative Action, vice-president for student services, Associate Dean). The contacted party will help the accuser resolve the complaint informally or help to draft a formal complaint.
2) *Investigation prior to formal action*: The purpose of this investigation is to establish whether there is a reasonable basis for believing that the violation has occurred.
3) *Process of taking formal action*: After deciding that there is a case and a negotiated settlement cannot be reached, formal action will be taken.
4) *Formal action*: Formal action will follow the proper procedure depending on the type of harasser (graduate assistant, student, or employee).
5) *Protection of complainant and others*: Issues of confidentiality and retaliation are discussed.
6) *Protection of the accused*: Confidentiality and false claims are discussed.
7) *Protecting both parties*: Confidentiality is emphasized and the fact that both parties will be informed promptly about the course and outcome of the proceedings.
8) *Educational programs*: The importance of educational efforts in this area is discussed. The Affirmative Action office is identified as re-

sponsible for distributing copies of the policy. The Affirmative Action office also develops series of training sessions for persons who are likely to receive complaints that this policy has been violated, i.e., Resident Assistants, academic advisors, etc. Academic departments are encouraged to train graduate assistants and other instructional personnel. The Affirmative Action office also is required to develop a course for those who inadvertently violate the sexual harassment policy.

Teachers College, Columbia University
525 West 120 St.
New York, NY 10027

Sexual Harassment Policy
Issued: November 1989
Revised: February 1992

Policy and Procedures (excerpt and description)

> Since Teachers College has long insisted upon a non-discriminatory policy in all domains of its activities, its position with regard to sexual harassment is unequivocal. The basic integrity of an institution of higher learning is threatened by a teacher who intimidates an junior colleague or a student by demanding sexual favors as a condition of academic advancement. A supervisor who harasses an employee and misuses a position of authority to achieve a private purpose is similarly corrupting. In short, sexual harassment by any Teachers College employee, faculty member, or student cannot and will not be tolerated. (Teachers College, Columbia University, 1992, p. 2)

The policy and procedures include the following features:

1) Reviews law; discusses power component and forms of sexual harassment; recommends speaking to offender first, and then taking a complaint to a member of the Sexual Harassment Panel (SHP).
2) Charge of the Sexual Harassment Panel (composed of faculty, staff, and students)—Describes who is involved, how they are appointed, and safety and confidentiality of the setting. The role of the SHP to provide guidance and counseling, assist in the resolution of complaints, and educate the community about sexual harassment.
3) Sexual harassment complaint procedures—informal and formal complaints

A) A complainant comes to an SHP member with a complaint, to report an incident, or to seek advice.

B) The SHP member obtains data through confidential discussion with the complainant.

C) The SHP member will give advice and guidance on both informal and formal procedures for resolving the problem.

D) If the case cannot be satisfactorily resolved through mediation or informal discussion, the complainant may initiate a formal investigation with the assistance of an SHP member.

4) Formal investigation

A) A formal investigation may be initiated in either of the following ways:

1. With assistance from an SHP member, a complainant files a formal grievance. This step may be taken at any time.

2. The complaint is addressed to either the Vice President for Academic Affairs (complaints against faculty or students) or the Vice President for Finance and Administration (complaints against staff), who will then designate the Panel to investigate the complaint.

B) All investigations of formal complaints will be conducted by the Panel or its representatives. In each instance, the Panel will report its findings, resolutions, and recommendations to the appropriate vice president.

C) The purpose of any recommended corrective action to resolve a complaint will be to correct or to remedy the injury, if any, to the complainant and to prevent further harassment. Recommended corrective action will reflect the level of sexual harassment involved.

Educational Resources – Organizations, Publications, Programs, and Curricular and Media Materials

Educational resources designed to address sexual harassment and related issues are listed below as a general group by organization, by educational level, and for parent education. Since few such resources have been developed for early childhood and elementary schools, I include some resources on sex stereotyping and gender bias. While I attempt to highlight those resources that appear to be most useful, there has been little formal assessment of their effectiveness. These resources and curricular materials should be reviewed by the reader to determine their appropriateness for a particular setting.

GENERAL

American Association of University Professors
1 Dupont Circle
Washington, DC 20036
Telephone: (202) 737-5900 (local)
(800) 424-2973 (long distance)
Fax: (202) 737-5526

The AAUP provides a policy and a procedure addressing sexual harassment, which may be used as a guide for developing sexual harassment policies and procedures. The Association has conducted a study of serious violations of sexual harassment guidelines on many AAUP-approved college campuses.

American Association of University Women (AAUW)
1111 16th Street NW

Washington, DC 20036-4873
Telephone: (202) 785-7788
Fax: (202) 872-1425

- *The AAUW Report: How Schools Shortchange Girls* (The American Association of University Women Educational Foundation and the National Education Association, 1992, Washington, DC: Author).
- *Hostile Hallways: The AAUW Survey on Sexual Harassment in America's Schools* (The American Association of University Women Educational Foundation, 1993, Washington, DC: Author).

These excellent publications explicate the issues of gender bias in American K–12 schools and sexual harassment in high schools. Both books contain important recommendations and provide educators with information for raising awareness and for designing educational programs on these issues.

American Federation of Teachers (AFT)

555 New Jersey Avenue NW
Washington, DC 20001
Telephone: (202) 879-4400 (general)
             (202) 879-4434 (Human Rights Department)
Fax: (202) 879-4502

- The *AFT Resource Guide*, prepared by the AFT Women's Rights Committee, is available to AFT faculty, locals, union members, and students. The guide covers the history, definition, myths, and facts about sexual harassment, and includes sample surveys and policies. It also focuses on specific topics such as suggestions for unions on addressing sexual harassment, sample contracts, and sample employer policies. The guide includes a bibliography of resources and describes sample workshops and scenarios for preventing and eliminating sexual harassment.

American Psychological Association

1200 17th Street NW
Washington, DC 20036
Telephone: (202) 336-5500

In the APA's Code of Ethics (1992), sexual harassment is clearly defined and stated as an unethical practice. Under this code, psychologists may not engage in sexual harassment. Violations can result in a formal review by the ethics committee.

The Center for Family Life Education
Planned Parenthood of Greater Northern New Jersey
575 Main Street
Hackensack, NJ 07601
Telephone: (201) 489-1265

The Center for Family Life Education consists of five resource centers throughout northern New Jersey. It supports the New Jersey State Family Life Education Mandate and offers various services for educating about interpersonal relations, family life, and human sexuality. It provides books, pamphlets, curricular materials for grades K–12, films and videos, workshops and conferences, inservice training programs for professionals, and programs for parents and students.

Center for Research on Women
Publications Department
Wellesley College
106 Central Street
Wellesley, MA 02181-8259
Telephone: (617) 283-2510

- *Secrets in Public: Sexual Harassment in Public (and Private) Schools.* Stein, N. (1993). Wellesley, MA: Wellesley College, Center for Research on Women.

This resource includes evidence from lawsuits and narratives from adolescent girls demonstrating the occurrence of student to student sexual harassment within schools, as well as adult to student sexual harassment and child abuse.

- *Secrets in Public: Sexual Harassment in our Schools.* Stein, N. D., Marshall, N. L., & Tropp, L. R. (1993). Wellesley, MA: Wellesley College, Center for Research on Women.

This publication presents the results of the *Seventeen* magazine survey, which included data on sexual harassment based on 2,002 surveys completed by girls of diverse racial backgrounds in grades 2–12.

Center for Women Policy Studies
2000 P Street NW
Suite 508
Washington, DC 20036

Telephone: (202) 872-1770
Fax: (202) 296-8962

- *In Case of Sexual Harassment: A Guide for Women Students*. Center for Women Policy Studies. (1992). Washington, DC: Author.

This brief guide is designed to provide college women with information regarding myths, definitions, types, effects, and examples of sexual harassment. It also includes examples of formal and informal grievance procedures.

Wisconsin Department of Public Instruction
Publication Sales
Drawer 179
Milwaukee, WI 53293-0179
Telephone: (800) 243-8782

- *Classroom Activities in Sex Equity for Developmental Guidance*. Wisconsin Department of Public Instruction. (1993). Milwaukee: Author.

This activity guide was designed for teachers and counselors, and serves to integrate sex-equity exercises into the classroom. Its approach works to eliminate bias, stereotyping, and discrimination based on gender. The program is structured to allow students in grades K–12 to master competencies during each stage of development, including elementary/primary grades, elementary/intermediate grades, middle/junior high grades, and high school grades. Three major areas of student development are highlighted: learning competencies, personal and social competencies, and career and vocational competencies.

Educational Equity Concepts, Inc. (EEC)
114 East 32nd Street
New York, NY 10016
Telephone: (212) 725-1803
Fax: (212) 725-0947

EEC is a national, nonprofit organization based in New York City. Its mission is to increase equity in education by reducing discrimination based on gender, race, ethnicity, and disability. To that end, EEC conducts training, workshops, and research, and develops and provides educational materials.

National Association of Independent Schools (NAIS)
Career Paths and Gender Equity Services
1620 L Street NW
Washington, DC 20036
Telephone: (202) 973-9700
Fax: (202) 973-9790

The NAIS packet of sexual harassment materials (available only for member organizations) is an excellent resource, which includes the NAIS policy on sexual harassment and policies for six member schools. Policy statements cover sexual harassment of employees and students, and may be helpful to schools attempting to develop their own policies and procedures. In addition, the packet includes a detailed issues paper, sample scenarios, and lists of useful resources.

National Council for Research on Women (NCRW)
530 Broadway at Spring Street, 10th floor
New York, NY 10012-3920
Telephone: (212) 274-0730
Fax: (212) 274-0821
email: MECHC@CUNYVM.EDU

NCRW member centers and institutes exist across the country and conduct research on women.

• *Sexual Harassment: Research and Resources* (1992), a report prepared by NCRW's Sexual Harassment Information Project, is a comprehensive document that includes sections on definition, impact on victims, sexual harassment and different groups of women, sexual harassment in schools, and policies and procedures.

National Education Association (NEA)
Human and Civil Rights Division
1201 Sixteenth Street NW
Washington, DC 20036-3290
Telephone: (202) 822-7700
Fax: (202) 822-7578

NEA provides a resource packet on student sexual harassment that includes a poster, pamphlets, and guides to help teenagers understand and address the issue. It also includes a sample policy and guidelines for training workshops and the development of policies.

The NEA has an additional resource packet for addressing workplace sexual harassment and student sexual harassment. The materials
include basic aspects of addressing sexual harassment (such as definition, effective policies, procedural and legal considerations, and the
responsibilities of those harassed, their supervisors, and management)
as well as a complete training format.

National Organization of Women—Legal Defense and Education Fund (NOW–LDEF)
99 Hudson Street
New York, NY 10013-2815
Telephone: (212) 925-6635
Fax: (212) 226-1066

* *Legal Resources Kit* (1992), prepared by NOW–LDEF, includes a general kit on sexual harassment in schools and one specific to administrators. The general *Legal Resources Kit* provides an overview of
  the problem, the provisions under Title IX, the procedure, a sample
  student complaint letter, and suggestions for action for schools and
  students.
  The *Legal Resources Kit* for elementary and secondary school administrators provides information about the relevant laws (Title VII
  and Title IX); guidelines for developing a sexual harassment policy
  and training programs for teachers, staff, and investigators; and additional resources.

United Federation of Teachers (UFT)
260 Park Avenue South
New York, NY 10010
Telephone: (212) 777-7500 (general)
              (212) 598-6861 (Women's Rights Committee)
Fax: (212) 677-6612

The Women's Rights Committee of the UFT has available useful
resource materials and sample policies pertaining to the issue of sexual
harassment in the workplace from various organizations. For instance,
the model sexual harassment policy of the New Jersey Community Relations Advisory Council (NJCRAC) includes a checklist of basic suggestions for handling sexual harassment complaints. The report of the
Michigan Task Force on Sexual Harassment in the Workplace presents a
good overview of how the task force developed and defined its work.

Women's Educational Equity Act (WEEA) Publishing Center
Education Development Center, Inc.
55 Chapel Street
Newton, MA 02160
Telephone: (617) 969-7100
          (800) 225-3088

The WEEA Publishing Center is a national clearinghouse and publisher of gender-fair educational materials that focus on reducing sex-role stereotyping in education.

• *WEEA Digest*, published by the WEEA Publication Center, discusses educational theory and research on gender equity in education and related issues such as gender-based violence and sexual harassment.

ELEMENTARY SCHOOL

• *Boys and Girls Together: Non-Sexist Activities for Elementary Schools.* Cain, M. A. (1980). Holmes Beach, FL: Learning Publications.

This publication offers a range of educational strategies in subject areas for eliminating sexism from classrooms. It includes illustrations, appendices of resources, and suggestions for how teachers can work with parents. It also offers guidelines teachers can use to conduct their own inservice training sessions for the school community.

Minnesota Department of Education
Equal Educational Opportunities
522 Capitol Square Building
550 Cedar Street
St. Paul, MN 55101
Telephone: (612) 296-7622

• *Girls and Boys Getting Along: Teaching Sexual Harassment Prevention.* Minnesota Department of Education. (1993). St. Paul, MN: Author.

This curriculum was developed for grades K–6, consisting of two separate programs for grades K–3 and 4–6. Its goal is the prevention and reduction of incidence of sexual harassment among students. The program includes activities related to personal safety, respecting others,

identifying sexual harassment, fostering positive gender-based relationships, and conflict resolution skills. It also provides information on laws
and policies to help educators prepare for the curriculum.

Rutgers University Press
109 Church Street
New Brunswick, NJ 08901
Telephone: (908) 932-7764

- *Learning About Family Life*. Sprung, B. (1992). New Brunswick, NJ:
  Rutgers University Press.

This curriculum, designed for grades K–3, addresses a range of issues pertaining to the family, human development and interpersonal
relations, responsible personal behavior, and sexuality and reproduction. The content of the curriculum is inclusive in terms of racial, ethnic, and socioeconomic diversity as well as physical disability, and sensitive to the issues of sex-role stereotyping and gender bias. While this
curriculum does not address the issue of sexual harassment *per se*, it is
designed with a view toward eliminating sexism from education in the
early years.

ETR Associates
P.O. Box 1830
Santa Cruz, CA 95061-1830
Telephone: (800) 321-4407

- *Resources for the Elementary Classroom (Grades 4, 5, 6)*. DeSpelder,
  L. A., & Strickland, A. L. (1982). Santa Cruz, CA: ETR Associates
  (Formerly Network Publications)

This resource was designed by Planned Parenthood of Santa Cruz
County for the Family Life Education Department of Health and Human
Services. It is to be used in combination with curricula for elementary
schools and includes activities focusing on such issues as interpersonal
relationships, communications skills, decision making, and human sexuality.

- *Touch Talk!* Berg, E. (1985). Santa Cruz: ETR Associates. (Grades
  K–2)
- *Stop It!* Berg, E. (1985). Santa Cruz: ETR Associates. (Grades 3–4)

* *Tell Someone!* Berg, E. (1985). Santa Cruz: ETR Associates. (Grades 5–6)

These small booklets address the difference between good and bad touches. They offer suggestions on how to confide in a trusted adult and what a child should do if someone touches him or her inappropriately.

MIDDLE AND SECONDARY SCHOOLS

ENABL—Education Now and Babies Later
Department of Health Services
Office of Family Planning
Health Education Section
714/744 P Street
P.O. Box 942732
Sacramento, CA 94234-7320
Telephone: (916)-654-0357
Fax: (916) 657-1608

The ENABL program was implemented by California to educate teenagers between the ages of 12 and 14 years (grades 7–9) to resist the pressure for sexual involvement before they feel ready for it. Using the *Postponing Sexual Involvement* educational materials (described later), the program educates young teenagers by discussing myths and facts about reproduction and sexually transmitted diseases, gender stereotyping, and sexual themes in the media. Five sessions are designed to equip teenagers with assertiveness techniques and strategies to resist pressure from peers and the media.

New Jersey Department of Education
Distribution Services
225 West State Street, CN 500
Trenton, NJ 08625

* *Family Life Education: Selected Programs and Practices in New Jersey Public Schools.* (1987).
* *Implementation of Family Life Education in New Jersey Public Schools.* (1986). New Jersey Department of Education. Trenton, NJ: Author.

These manuals provide overviews of the implementation of the Family Life Education mandate in New Jersey. They include brief descriptions of curriculum models that exist in public schools throughout New Jersey and discuss promising programs and implementation problems. The educational programs include teaching about human development and sexuality, responsible personal decision making, family life, and interpersonal relationships.

Wellesley College Center for Research on Women
106 Central Street
Wellesley, MA 02181-8259
Telephone: (617) 283-2500
Fax: (617) 283-2504

- *Flirting or Hurting?: A Teacher's Guide on Student-to-Student Harassment in Schools.* Stein, N., & Sjostrom, L. (1994). Washington, DC: National Education Association and Wellesley College, Center for Research on Women.

This resource's goal is to assist students in grades 6–12 in understanding the meaning of personal choice and social responsibility. The curricular materials address the importance of standing up to sexual harassment and also include sections on dating violence, racial and ethnic intolerance, gay bashing, and so on. The program involves the use of age-appropriate materials for grades 6–12. It emphasizes multiple training sessions for all individuals (teachers, administrators, cafeteria workers, bus drivers, teacher's aides, janitors, coaches, etc.), in addition to parent and guardian involvement.

Minnesota Department of Education
Equal Educational Opportunities
522 Capitol Square Building
550 Cedar Street
St. Paul, MN 55101
Telephone: (612) 296-7622

- *It's* Not *Fun, It's Illegal: The Identification and Prevention of Sexual Harassment to Teenagers: A Curriculum.* Minnesota Department of Education. (1993). St. Paul, MN: Author.

This curriculum is designed for use with junior and senior high school students. The authors recommend that teachers examine and understand their own attitudes, values, and comfort levels before discussing sexual harassment with their students. The publication also includes several handouts and transparencies (for example, showing why and how to write a letter to a harasser), case studies, surveys, a sample policy, and a questionnaire.

Natural Helpers
Georgia Department of Education
Equity Unit
1854 Twin Towers East
Atlanta, GA 30334-5060
Telephone: (404) 656-2540

Natural Helpers is a group of seventh and eighth graders who work toward educating peers about sexual harassment in middle schools. The group produced a video that explains what could be considered sexual harassment in school settings.

Postponing Sexual Involvement
Teen Services Program
Grady Memorial Hospital
Box 26158
80 Butler Street, SE
Atlanta, GA 30335-3801
Telephone: (404) 616-3513

Postponing Sexual Involvement, developed by the Emory/Grady Teen Services Program in Atlanta, Georgia, is a sex education program established for 13- to 15-year-olds. Its aim is to help students resist peer and social pressures to engage in sexual activity. Studies indicate that the program is informative and effective (Howard & McCabe, 1990).

- *Resources for Educational Equity: A Guide for Grades Pre-Kindergarten–12.* Froschl, M., & Sprung, B. (1988). New York: Garland.

This resource includes annotated lists of picture books, classroom materials, a video, and teacher resources for equity in education, including gender equity. It offers valuable teaching strategies and suggests that from the middle grades onward students can analyze media messages and advertisements and explore the historic and economic foundations of negative stereotypes.

The *Teachable Moments* video and its accompanying manual prepare leaders to implement the program, and provide systematic teaching strategies and useful suggestions about classroom climate.

Free Spirit Publishing
400 First Avenue North
Suite 616
Minneapolis, MN 55401
Telephone: (612) 338-2068

- *Sexual Harassment and Teens: A Program for Positive Change.* Strauss, S., Marshall, N. L., & Tropp, L. R. (1993). Minneapolis, MN: Free Spirit.

This curricular program for teenagers and students in grades 7–12 is an excellent resource for teachers. It provides a very useful curricular framework along with thoughtful, practical suggestions for implementation. A section on supporting victims of sexual harassment would be helpful to peer educators, school counselors, and parents.

Programs for Educational Opportunity
1005 School of Education
The University of Michigan
Ann Arbor, MI 48109-1259
Telephone: (313) 763-9910
Fax: (313) 763-1229

- *Tune in to Your Rights . . . A Guide for Teenagers About Turning Off Sexual Harassment.* Center for Sex Equity in Schools. (1985). Ann Arbor: University of Michigan.

This guide helps teenagers recognize and deal with sexual harassment they may encounter in their high school settings. The style, layout, and language of this publication are designed to appeal to teenagers and to provide them with useful information.

Massachusetts Department of Education
Instruction and Curriculum Services
350 Main Street
Malden, MA 02148-5023
Telephone: (617) 388-3300

- *Who's Hurt and Who's Liable: Sexual Harassment in Massachusetts Schools: A Curriculum and Guide for School Personnel.* Klein, F., & Wilber, N. (1986). Quincy: Massachusetts Department of Education.

This comprehensive resource offers useful curricular materials, including discussions of the definition of sexual harassment, underlying societal norms, legal issues, and administrative strategies. A range of strategies are presented, such as establishing student support groups and implementing a range of disciplinary actions and training programs for teachers, school personnel, and administrators.

HIGHER EDUCATION

Massachusetts Institute of Technology
77 Massachusetts Avenue
Cambridge, MA 02139
Telephone: (617) 253-1000

- *Fight Back!!! An Underground Guide to Fighting Sexual Harassment.* Graduate Student News. (1991). Cambridge: Massachusetts Institute of Technology.

This guide includes answers to questions such as how to get immediate support and how to stop harassment, and also provides an extensive list of resources at MIT and off campus.

The Feminist Press at City University of New York
311 East 94th Street
New York, NY 10128
Telephone: (212) 360-5794
Fax: (212) 348-1241

- *Get Smart! What You Should Know (But Won't Learn in Class) About Sexual Harassment and Sex Discrimination.* Katz, M., & Vieland, V. (1991). New York: Feminist Press.

This book serves as a resource for female college students. It describes issues and disadvantages women face in higher education and offers ways to combat sexual harassment in and out of school. Case studies as well as civil rights and discrimination laws are included.

Office of the Attorney General, Minnesota
102 State Capitol
St. Paul, MN 55155

Telephone: (612) 296-6196
            (800) 657-3787 (TDD or voice)
Fax: (612) 297-4193

• *Review and Comment on Campus Plans to Prevent Violence and Sexual Harassment.* Office of the Attorney General and The Higher Education Coordinating Board. (1993). St. Paul, MN: Authors.

This publication cites useful examples of education and training programs at various institutions of higher education, ranging from lectures and forums, to counseling and formal curricula that address issues of sexual harassment and violence. It details aspects of campus safety and security, such as landscaping, lighting, and security telephones, that institutions need to consider carefully. In addition, it provides a general framework for developing campus plans to address sexual harassment.

National Education Association
Office of Higher Education
1201 Sixteenth Street NW
Washington, DC 20036-3290
Telephone: (202) 833-4000

• *Sexual Harassment in Higher Education: Concepts and Issues.* Fitzgerald, L. F. (1992). Washington, DC: National Education Association.

This booklet provides a history of the problem of sexual harassment, a definition of sexual harassment, a discussion of the legal context and cases, and consensual amorous relationships, and includes examples of campus policies and procedures. It is aimed at assisting campus administrators, faculty, staff, students, and union leaders with the issue of sexual harassment.

American Council on Education (ACE)
Publications Department
One Dupont Circle
Washington, DC 20036

• *Sexual Harassment on Campus.* American Council on Education. (1992). Washington, DC: Author.

This guide, published by ACE, addresses the importance of establishing effective sexual harassment programs on university campuses. It discusses the process of developing sexual harassment programs, includ-

ing sexual harassment definitions, sample policies and grievance procedures, and a discussion of the essential components of an effective sexual harassment program.

The following institutions of higher education are examples of
those that have developed materials and work on sexual harassment:

Cornell University
Office of Equal Opportunity
234 Day Hall
Ithaca, NY 14853-2801
Telephone: (607) 255-3976
TDD: (607) 255-7665

Hofstra University
Department of Administration and Policy Studies
124 Hofstra University
208 Mason Hall
Hempstead, NY 11560
Telephone: (516) 463-5758

Johns Hopkins University
Ombuds Office
3400 North Charles Street
Nichols House
Baltimore, MD 21218
Telephone: (410) 516-5300

Massachusetts Institute of Technology
Ombuds Office Room 10-213
77 Massachusetts Avenue
Cambridge, MA 02139-4307
Telephone: (617) 253-5921

Princeton University
Sexual Harassment/Assault Advising, Resources and Education
(SHARE)
McCosh Health Center
Princeton, NJ 08540
Telephone: (609) 258-3310

Syracuse University
Office of Human Resources
Skytop Office Building
Syracuse, NY 13244-5300
Telephone: (315) 433-2488
Fax: (315) 433-1063

Teachers College, Columbia University

Associate Dean's Office
Box 151
Teachers College, Columbia
  University
New York, NY 10027
Telephone: (212) 678-3052

Office of Personnel Services
Box 149
Teachers College, Columbia
  University
New York, NY 10027
Telephone: (212) 678-3175

PARENT EDUCATION

Center for Adolescent Reproductive Health at Emory University/Grady Memorial Hospital
Box 26158
80 Butler Street, SE
Atlanta, GA 30335-3801
Telephone: (404) 616-3513

- *How to Help Your Teenager Postpone Sexual Involvement.* Howard, M. (1989). New York: Continuum.

This book, designed for parents as well as professionals who work with parents and/or youth, aims at helping parents to understand the social and peer pressures young people experience with regard to becoming sexually active. The resource assists parents in increasing their ability to communicate with their teens about postponing sexual involvement.

Planned Parenthood of Westchester and Rockland, Inc.
Training and Resource Center
175 Tarrytown Road
White Plains, NY 10607

- *Straight Talk.* Ratner, M., & Chamlin, S. (1985). New York: Penguin Books.

This resource includes information and advice for parents in communicating with their children about sexuality. It includes activities to encourage conversation about such topics as parts of the body, family life, and sex roles.

Planned Parenthood of Lane County
Health Services of Southwestern Oregon
1670 High Street
Eugene, OR 97401
Telephone: (503) 344-2632
Fax: (503) 344-6519

- *There's No Place Like Home . . . for Sex Education.* Widoff, M. (1989). Eugene, OR: Planned Parenthood Association of Lane County.

This program aims to assist parents in educating children about sexual attitudes, behaviors, and lifestyles, and emphasizes the role of parents as primary educators of their children. Five newsletters are available for every age/grade level, from preschool through grade 12.

MEDIA MATERIAL

There are a number of audiovisual resources addressing sexual harassment and related issues, including date rape and sexual abuse. The examples below suggest the range of resources available.

California State Department of Education
Project Sex Equity in Education
721 Capitol Mall
Sacramento, CA 94244-2720
Telephone: (916) 657-2451

- *It's Not Funny . . . If It Hurts, for Students* (nd, 10 minutes)

This filmstrip was developed for students and deals with sexual harassment in California public schools.

- *Think About It . . . It Won't Go Away* (nd, 10 minutes)

This filmstrip was developed for administrators, counselors, and teachers, and deals with sexual harassment in California public schools.

NEA Professional Library
Box 509
West Haven, CT 06515
Telephone: (800) 229-4200

- *Sexual Harassment in Schools* (nd, 15 minutes)

This videotape was published by the National Education Association and the Learning Channel.

Massachusetts Department of Education
350 Main Street
Malden, MA 02148-5023
Telephone: (617) 388-3300

- *No Laughing Matter: High School Students and Sexual Harassment* (1982, 25 minutes)

This video or slide/tape, accompanied by a user's guide, was published by Media Works, Inc. and the Boston Women's Teacher Group. It depicts the experiences of three high school women who encounter sexual harassment in school and in the workplace.

Affirmative Action Office, AD 301
State University of New York at Albany
1400 Washington Avenue
Albany, NY 12222
Telephone: (518) 442-5415

- *Your Right to Fight: Stopping Sexual Harassment on Campus* (1989, 38 minutes)

This video was developed and produced by students and faculty at the State University of New York at Albany. It focuses on several cases of sexual harassment in higher education and analyzes the process of building up a case and filing a complaint.

Department of Psychology
State University of New York at Albany
1400 Washington Avenue
Albany, NY 12222
Telephone: (518) 442-3300

- *Take Back the Day: Stopping Peer Harassment on Campus* (nd)

This video addresses peer sexual harassment using student role models. Its goals include aiming to dispel myths, promoting assertive behavior, and teaching tactics to fight sexual harassment.

Media Services—Audio-Visual
Comstock Hall
Cornell University
Ithaca, NY 14853
Telephone: (607) 255-2091

- *Stop Date Rape: How to Get What You Want But Not More Than You Bargained For* (1987, 23 minutes)

This resource, which includes a teacher's guide, uses theater to stimulate discussion among students about date rape and strategies for preventing it.

Extension Media Center
University of California at Berkeley
2000 Center Street
Berkeley, CA 94720
Telephone: (510) 642-0460

- *Surviving Sexual Abuse* (1987, 27 minutes)

This video involves four young adult survivors of child sexual abuse (two men and two women) who share their experiences of betrayal and healing.

Counseling Services (Student Relationship Violence Committee)
State University of New York, College at Brockport
Brockport, NY 14420
Telephone: (716) 395-2211

- *Valentines and Violence* (1987, 59 minutes)

This video examines physical and verbal violence in dating relationships.

Federal Organizations and Selected Laws Related to Sexual Harassment and Schools

The Office for Civil Rights and Title IX
U.S. Department of Education—Office for Civil Rights
330 C Street SW
Washington, DC 20202-1328
Telephone: (202) 205-5813
Fax: (202) 205-9862

The Office for Civil Rights (OCR) in the Department of Education is responsible for ensuring that institutions comply with Title IX, as described in Chapters 1 and 2. The OCR provides guidance and support to assist institutions in complying with the law. It informs beneficiaries of Title IX, including students and applicants for admission to academic programs, of their rights. Publications include:

1) *Sexual Harassment: It's Not Academic* (U.S. Department of Education, September 1988, Washington, DC)
2) *Title IX and Sex Discrimination* (U.S. Department of Education, November 1987, Washington, DC)
3) *Title IX Grievance Procedures: An Introductory Manual* (U.S. Department of Education, 1987, Washington, DC)

Regional Offices of the Office for Civil Rights:

Region I
(CT, ME, MA, NH, RI, VT)
Office for Civil Rights, Region I
U.S. Department of Education
John W. McCormack Post Office and Court House
Room 222—Post Office Square

Boston, MA 02109
(617) 223-1154 TTY (617) 223-1111

Region II
(NJ, NY, Puerto Rico, Virgin Islands)
Office for Civil Rights, Region II
U.S. Department of Education
26 Federal Plaza—33rd Floor
New York, NY 10278
(212) 264-5180 TTY (212) 264-9464

Region III
(DE, MD, PA, VA, WV, Washington DC)
Office for Civil Rights, Region III
U.S. Department of Education
Gateway Building—3535 Market Street
Room 6300—Post Office Box 13716
Philadelphia, PA 19101
(215) 596-6787 TTY (215) 596-6794

Region IV
(AL, FL, GA, KY, MS, NC, SC, TN)
Office for Civil Rights, Region IV
U.S. Department of Education
101 Marietta Tower—Room 2702
Atlanta, GA 30323
(404) 221-2954 TTY (404) 221-3322

Region V
(IL, IN, MI, MN, OH, WI)
Office for Civil Rights, Region V
U.S. Department of Education
300 South Wacker Drive—8th Floor
Chicago, IL 60606
(312) 886-3456 TTY (312) 353-2540

Region VI
(AR, LO, NM, OK, TX)
Office for Civil Rights, Region VI
U.S. Department of Education
1200 Main Tower—Room 1420
Dallas, TX 75202
(816) 844-5695 TTY (816) 374-7264

Region VII
(IA, KS, MO, NE)
Office for Civil Rights, Region VII
U.S. Department of Education
324 East 11th Street—24th Floor
Kansas City, MO 64106
(816) 374-2223 TTY (816) 374-7264

Region VIII
(CO, MT, ND, SD, UT, WY)
Office for Civil Rights, Region VIII
U.S. Department of Education
Federal Office Building
1961 Stout Street—Room 342
Denver, CO 80294
(303) 844-5695 TTY (303) 844-3417

Region IX
(AZ, CA, HI, NV, American Samoa, Guam, Trust Territory of
the Pacific Islands)
Office for Civil Rights, Region IX
U.S. Department of Education
1275 Market Street—14th Floor
San Francisco, CA 94103
(415) 556-9894 TTY (415) 556-1933

Region X
(AK, ID, OR, WA)
Office for Civil Rights, Region X
U.S. Department of Education
2901 3rd Avenue—MS/106—1st Floor
Seattle, WA 98121
(206) 442-1636 TTY (206) 442-4542

THE DESEGREGATION ASSISTANCE CENTERS (DACs)

There are 10 DACs across the United States, which are funded under Title IV of the Civil Rights Act to provide elementary and secondary
schools with services to increase equity in terms of race, gender, and
national origin. Services may include technical assistance, on-site training, and planning assistance to school districts, and resources on sexual

harassment in education. Each of the 10 DACs can be contacted to obtain a list of the specific services they offer to schools within their respective regions.

Title IV Desegregation Assistance Centers (DAC):

Region I
(CT, ME, MA, NH, RI, VT)
New England Desegregation Assistance Center
Brown University
144 Wayland Avenue
Providence, RI 02926
Office: (401) 351-7577
Fax: (401) 421-7650

Region II
(NJ, NY, Puerto Rico, Virgin Islands)
The Metro Center
32 Washington Place, Suite 72
New York, NY 10003
Office: (212) 998-5100
Fax: (212) 995-4199

Region III
(DE, MD, PA, VA, WV, Washington, DC)
Mid-Atlantic Center
5454 Wisconsin Ave., Suite 1500
Chevy Chase, MD 20815
Office: (301) 657-7741
Fax: (301) 657-8782

Region IV
(AL, FL, GA, KY, MS, NC, SC, TN)
Southeastern Desegregation Assistance Center
Miami Equity Associates, Inc.
8603 S. Dixie Highway, Suite 304
Miami, FL 33143
Office: (305) 669-0114
Fax: (305) 669-9809

Region V
(IL, IN, MI, MN, OH, WI)
Regents of the University of Michigan
4725 E. Jefferson St., Rm. 1322, U-M
Ann Arbor, MI 48109
Office: (313) 763-9901
Fax: (313) 763-1229

Region VI
(AR, LO, NM, OK, TX)
Intercultural Development Research Association
5835 Callahan, Suite 350
San Antonio, TX 78210
Office: (512) 684-8180
Fax: (512) 684-5389

Region VII
(IA, KS, MO, NE)
Midwest Desegregation Assistance Center
Kansas State University, Bluemont Hall
Manhattan, KS 66506
Office: (913) 532-6408
Fax: (913) 532-7304

Region VIII
(CO, MT, ND, SD, UT, WY)
Metropolitan State College/Denver
1100 Stout Street, Suite 800
Denver, CO 80204
Office: (303) 556-2999
Fax: (303) 556-8505

Region IX
(AZ, CA, NV)
Southwest Regional Laboratory
4665 Lampson Avenue
Los Alamitos, CA 90720
Office: (310) 598-7661
Fax: (310) 985-9635

Region X
(AK, HI, ID, OR, WA, American Samoa, Guam, Northern Mariana, Trust Territories)
Northwest Regional Education Laboratory
101 SW Main Street, Suite 500
Portland, OR 97204
Office: (503) 275-9507
Fax: (503) 275-9489

The Equal Employment Opportunity Commission (EEOC)
Office of Equal Employment Opportunity
1801 L Street NW
Washington, DC 20507
Telephone: (202) 663-4900 (local)
              (202) 663-4494 (TDD local)
              (800) 669-EEOC (long distance)
              (800) 800-3302 (TDD long distance)

The EEOC enforces Title VII of the Civil Rights Act of 1964, which prohibits employment discrimination based on race, color, religion, sex, or national origin. The EEOC has 23 district, 1 field, 17 area, and 9 local offices located throughout the country.

SELECTED LAWS RELATED TO SEXUAL HARASSMENT AND SCHOOLS

The *Family Educational Rights and Privacy Act of 1974* (FERPA) [can be cited as "Education Amendments of 1974" and 20 USC 1232g] has two major goals: to guarantee students and their families access to their education records, and to protect students' privacy by limiting access to records. The act applies to all educational institutions that receive federal funds. It states that schools cannot deny parents "the right to inspect and review any and all official records, files and data directly related to their children" (Sec. 438(a)(1)), and that "Parents shall have an opportunity for a hearing to challenge the content of their child's school records" (Sec. 438(a)(2)). It further denies funding to any educational institution that releases personally identifiable student records or files, including disciplinary records, without the written consent of their parents except to a few specified school and government officials. Student records that may include incidents of sexual harassment are not available to the press or to other students. However, such records may be released to other schools to which a student is applying with notification to the parents.

The *Student Right to Know and Campus Security Act of 1990* (20 USC 1092f) amends FERPA, addressing the rights of victims of violent crimes. Specifically, it provides an exemption to FERPA, that victims of sexual assault be notified of the outcome of disciplinary proceedings. Schools must notify an alleged victim of sexual assault as to whether, for example, the accused was found guilty and expelled. The act further mandates that schools "prepare, publish and distribute, through appropriate publications or mailings, to all current students and employees, and to any applicant for enrollment or employment upon request, an annual security report" (sec. 204(f)) which includes statistics on a variety of crimes, and on campus security practices. This reporting includes on-campus crime as well as crime in "any building or property owned or controlled by student organizations recognized by the institution" (Sec. 204(5)(B)), including off-campus fraternities and sororities. The act requires that schools annually publicize the extent of more severe forms of sexual harassment, including incidents in off-campus, school-affiliated buildings and grounds.

The *Violence Against Women Act of 1994* (VAWA) (42 USC 40281-40703) makes it possible for victims of crimes based upon gender, including rape and battery, to sue for violation of civil rights. The principle of the act is "to protect the civil rights of victims of gender motivated violence and to promote public safety, health, and activities affecting interstate commerce by establishing a Federal civil rights cause of action for victims of crimes of violence motivated by gender" (Sec. 40302). Significantly, such suits would be tried in civil court where the plaintiff needs to prove a preponderance of evidence standard (rather than the more difficult beyond a reasonable doubt standard of criminal court). Suits may seek compensatory relief and punitive damages, may recover attorney fees, and the court may award injunctive relief (i.e., stay-away orders). The VAWA also provides funding for a variety of programs, including programs to: educate judges, educate youth, help states and localities combat violence against women, and raise funds for battered-women shelters. This act provides an additional avenue of recourse to victims of some forms of sexual harassment.

References

Adams, J. W., Kottke, J. L., & Padgitt, J. S. (1983). Sexual harassment of university students. *Journal of College Student Personnel, 24*, 484–490.

Alexander v. Yale University, D.C. Conn. 1977, 459 F. Supp. 1, *aff'd* 631 F.2d 178 (2nd Cir. 1980).

American Association of University Professors. (1995). *Sexual harassment: Suggested policy and procedures for handling complaints.* Washington, DC: Author.

American Association of University Women. (1992). *The AAUW report: How schools shortchange girls.* Washington, DC: Author

American Association of University Women. (1993). *Hostile hallways: The AAUW survey on sexual harassment in America's schools.* Washington, DC: Author.

American Heritage Dictionary of the English Language (3rd ed.) (1992). Boston: Houghton Mifflin.

American Psychological Association. (1992). *Code of ethics, standard 1.11.* Washington, DC: Author.

American Psychological Association Ethics Committee. (1994). Report of the ethics committee, 1993. *American Psychologist, 49*(7), 659–666.

Annese, J. (1995, December 4). C.U. faculty react to draft of harassment procedures. *The Cornell Daily Sun*, pp. 1, 10.

Aurelia D. v. Monroe County Board of Education, No. 94-140-4-MAC (WDO) (M.D. Ga. Aug. 29, 1994).

Banks, J. A. (1995). Multicultural education: Its effects on students' racial and gender role attitudes. In J. A. Banks & C. A. McGee Banks (Eds.), *Handbook of research on multicultural education* (pp. 617–627). New York: Macmillan.

Barnard, W. A., & Benn, M. S. (1988). Belief congruence and prejudice reduction in an interracial contact setting. *The Journal of Social Psychology, 128*(1), 125–134.

Beauvais, K. (1986). Workshops to combat sexual harassment: A case study of changing attitudes. *Signs: Journal of Women in Culture and Society, 12*(1), 130–145.

Bell, S. T., Kuriloff, P. J., Lottes, I., Nathanson, J., Judge, T., & Fogelson-Turet, K. (1992). Rape callousness in college freshman: An investigation of the sociocultural model of aggression towards women. *Journal of College Student Development, 33*, 454–461.

Bem, D. J. (1968). Attitudes as self-descriptions: Another look at the attitude–

behavior link. In A. Greenwald, T. Brock, & T. Ostrom (Eds.), *Psychological foundations of attitudes* (pp. 197–215). New York: Academic Press.

Benson, D., Charlton, C., & Goodhart, F. (1992). Acquaintance rape on campus: A literature review. *Journal of American College Health, 40,* 157–165.

Benson, D. J., & Thomson, G. E. (1982). Sexual harassment on a university campus: The confluence of authority relations, sexual interest and gender stratification. *Social Problems, 290,* 236–251.

Benson, K. (1984). Comment on Crocker's "An analysis of university definitions of sexual harassment." *Signs: Journal of Women in Culture and Society, 9*(3), 516–519.

Berkowitz, A. (1992). College men as perpetrators of acquaintance rape and sexual assault: A review of recent research. *Journal of American College Health, 40,* 175–181.

Bogart, K., & Stein, N. (1987). Breaking the silence: Sexual harassment in education. *Peabody Journal of Education, 64*(4), 146–163.

Bohmer, C., & Parrot, A. (1993). *Sexual assault on campus: The problem and the solution.* New York: Lexington Books.

Botvin, G. J., Baker, E., Dugenbury, L., Botvin, E. M., & Diaz, T. (1995). Long-term follow-up results of a randomized drug abuse prevention trial in a white middle-class population. *Journal of the American Medical Association, 273*(14), 1106–1112.

Bourque, L. B. (1989). *Defining rape.* London: Duke University Press.

Brandenburg, J. B. (1982). Sexual harassment in the university: Guidelines for establishing a grievance procedure. *Signs: Journal of Women in Culture and Society, 8,* 320–336.

Brandenburg, J. B. (1994a). *Survey of sexual harassment policies, procedures, and educational initiatives at New York State research universities with schools of education.* Unpublished report.

Brandenburg, J. B. (1994b). [Survey of teacher preparation faculty on issue of sexual harassment]. Unpublished raw data.

Brandenburg, J. B. (1995). *Sexual harassment: A challenge to schools of education.* Washington, DC: American Association of Colleges for Teacher Education.

Bridges, J. S. (1993). Pink or blue: Gender-stereotypic perceptions of infants as conveyed by birth congratulations cards. *Psychology of Women Quarterly, 17,* 193–205.

Briere, J., & Malamuth, N. M. (1983). Self-reported likelihood of sexually aggressive behavior: Attitudinal versus sexual explanations. *Journal of Research in Personality, 17,* 315–323.

Brown, W.A., & Maestro-Scherer, J. (1986). *Assessing sexual harassment and public safety: A survey of Cornell women.* Unpublished report, Cornell Office of Equal Opportunity.

Bundy v. Jackson, 641 F.2d 934 (D.C. Cir. 1981).

Burt, M. R. (1980). Cultural myths and supports for rape. *Journal of Personality and Social Psychology, 38*(2), 217–230.

Byrnes, D. A., & Kiger, G. (1990). The effect of a prejudice-reduction simulation on attitude change. *Journal of Applied Social Psychology*, 20(4), 341–356.

Calder, B. J., & Ross, M. (1973). *Attitudes and behavior*. Morristown, NJ: General Learning Press.

California State Department of Education. (1992). *General Education Code Provisions, §212.6: Educational institutions; written policy on sexual harassment*. Sacramento, CA: Author.

Cannon v. University of Chicago, 441 U.S. 677 (1979).

Carr, R. A. (1991). Addicted to power: Sexual harassment and the unethical behavior of university faculty. *Canadian Journal of Counseling, 25*(4), 447–461.

Celis, W., 3d. (1991, January 2). Students trying to draw line between sex and an assault. *The New York Times*, pp. A1, B8.

Check, J. V. P., & Malamuth, N. M. (1983). Sex role stereotyping and reactions to depictions of stranger versus acquaintance rape. *Journal of Personality and Social Psychology, 45*(2), 344–356.

City School District of the City of New York. (1988). *Procedure for complaints of alleged discrimination by students, parents of students, and employees, including complaints of sexual harassment*. New York: Author.

Cleveland, J. N., & Kerst, J. N. (1993). Sexual harassment and perceptions of power: An under-articulated relationship. *Journal of Vocational Behavior, 42*, 49-67.

Columbia College. (1993). *If you have sexual harassment problems tell someone!* (Brochure issued by the Dean's Office and the Student Committee on Coeducational Affairs).

Columbia loses harassment suit. (1996, February 15). *The New York Times*, p. B8.

Commonwealth of Massachusetts. (1981). *Sexual harassment policy and procedure*. Malden, MA: Author.

Cortines, R. (1995, June 18). [Interview aired on CBS radio].

Crull, P. (1991). The stress effects of sexual harassment on the job. In M. A. Paludi & R. B. Barickman (Eds.), *Academic and workplace sexual harassmen: A resource journal* (pp. 133–144). Albany: State University of New York Press.

Davis, D. M. (1990). Portrayals of women in prime-time network television: Some demographic characteristics. *Sex Roles, 23*, 325–332.

DeFour, D. C. (1990). The interface of racism and sexism on college campuses. In M. A. Paludi (Ed.), *Ivory power: Sexual harassment on campus* (pp. 45–52). Albany: State University of New York Press.

De Gaston, J. F., Jensen, L., Weed, S. E., & Tanas, R. (1994). Teacher philosophy and program implementation and the impact on sex education outcomes. *Journal of Research and Development in Education, 27*(4), 265–270.

DeSpelder, L. A., & Strickland, A. L. (1982). *Resources for the Elementary Classroom* (grades 4, 5, 6). Santa Cruz, CA: ETR Associates.

Dey, E. L., Sax, L. J., & Korn, J. (1994, April). *Betrayed by the academy: The sexual harassment of women college faculty*. Paper presented at the annual meeting of the American Educational Research Association, New Orleans.

Doe v. Petaluma City School District, No. C-93-0123 EFL (N.D. Calif. 1993).

Douglas, W. (1993, August 26). Students bring $6M sex-harass lawsuit. *New York Newsday*, p. 15.

Dziech, B. W., & Weiner, L. (1990). *The lecherous professor: Sexual harassment on campus*. Chicago: University of Illinois Press.

East Side Union High School District, 09-93-1293-I, Nov. 9, 1993.

Eaton, S. (1993, July/August). Sexual harassment at an early age: New cases are changing the rules for schools. *The Harvard Education Letter*, pp. 1–4.

Eden Prairie, Minnesota, OCR 05-92-1194, May 1992.

Educators Guide to Controlling Sexual Harassment. (1993). Washington, DC: Thompson Publishing Group.

Enns, C. Z., McNeilly, C. L., Corkery, J. M., & Gilbert, M. S. (1995). The debate about delayed memories of child sexual abuse: A feminist perspective. *The Counseling Psychologist, 23*(2), 181–279.

Equal Employment Opportunity Commission. (1980). *Guidelines on discrimination because of sex*, 29 C.F.R. § 1604.11.

Equal Employment Opportunity Commission. (1990, March 19). *Policy guidance on current issues of sexual harassment*. Notice N-915-050.

Eskenazi, M., & Gallen, D. (1992). *Sexual harassment: Know your rights*. New York: Carroll & Graf.

Fain, T. C., & Anderton, D. L. (1987). Organized contexts and diffuse states. *Sex Roles, 17*, 291–311.

Festinger, L. (1957). *A theory of cognitive dissonance*. Evanston, IL: Peterson.

Fishbein, M., & Ajzen, I. (1975). *Belief, attitude, intention and behavior: An introduction to theory and research*. Reading, MA: Addison-Wesley.

Fitzgerald, L. F. (1992, May). *The last great open secret: The sexual harassment of women in academia and the workplace*. Address sponsored by the Federation of Behavioral, Psychological and Cognitive Sciences, Washington, DC.

Fitzgerald, L. F., & Shullman, S. L. (1993). Sexual harassment: A research analysis and agenda for the 1990s. *Journal of Vocational Behavior, 42*, 5–27.

Fitzgerald, L. F., Shullman, S. L., Bailey, N., Richards, M., Swecker, J., Gold, Y., Ormerod, M., & Weitzman, L. (1988). The incidence and dimensions of sexual harassment in academia and the workplace. *Journal of Vocational Behavior, 32*, 152–175.

Franklin v. Gwinnet County Public Schools, 112 S.Ct. 1028 (1992).

Fried, J. P. (1991, October 26). St. John's senior in assault case gets suspension. *The New York Times*, p. A23.

Froschl, M., & Sprung, B. (1988). *Resources for educational equity: A guide for grades pre-kindergarten–12*. New York: Garland.

Furuto, S. B. C. L. & Furuto, D. M. (1983). The effects of affective and cognitive treatment on attitude change toward ethnic minority groups. *International Journal of Intercultural Relations, 7,* 149–165.

Garner, H. (1995). *The first stone.* Sydney: Picador-Pan Macmillan Australia.

Gilbert, B. J., Heesacker, M., & Gannon, L. J. (1991). Changing the sexual aggression-supportive attitudes of men: A psychoeducational intervention. *Journal of Counseling Psychology, 38*(2), 197–203.

Goldberg, C. (1995a, May 11). Teacher and girl: A step ahead of the law. *The New York Times,* B1, B8.

Goldberg, C. (1995b, August 3). Company to pay record amount in L.I. sexual harassment case. *The New York Times,* A1, D8.

Goodwin, M. P., Roscoe, B., Rose, M., & Repp, S. E. (1989). Sexual harassment: Experiences of university employees. *Initiatives, 52*(3), 25–33.

Greenhouse, L. (1993, November 10). Court, 9–0, makes sex harassment easier to prove. *The New York Times,* pp. A1, A22.

Gross, J. (1993a, March 29). Where "boys will be boys," and adults are befuddled. *The New York Times,* A1, A13.

Gross, J. (1993b, September 25). Combating rape on campus in a class on sexual consent. *The New York Times,* pp. A1, A9.

Gross, J. (1994, January 16). Sex educators for young see new virtue in chastity. *The New York Times,* pp. A1, A13.

Gruber, J. E., Smith, M., & Kauppinen-Toropainen, K. (1996). Sexual harassment types and severity: Linking research and policy. In M. S. Stockdale (Ed.), *Sexual harassment in the workplace* (pp. 151–173). Thousand Oaks, CA: Sage.

Gutek, B. A. (1985). *Sex and the workplace.* San Francisco: Jossey-Bass.

Gutek, B. A., & Koss, M. P. (1993). Changed women and changed organizations: Consequences of and coping with sexual harassment. *Journal of Vocational Behavior, 42,* 28–48.

Gutek, B. A., & Morasch, B. (1982). Sex-ratios, sex-role spillover, and sexual harassment of women at work. *Journal of Social Issues, 38*(4), 55–74.

Hall, R., & Sandler, B. (1982). *The classroom climate: A chilly one for women?* Paper written for the Project on the Status and Education of Women, Association of American Colleges, Washington, DC.

Hanisch, K. A. (1996). An integrated framework for studying the outcomes of sexual harassment: Consequences for individuals and organizations. In M. S. Stockdale (Ed.), *Sexual harassment in the workplace* (pp. 174–198). Thousand Oaks, CA: Sage.

Harris v. Forklift Systems, Inc., No. 92-1168 S.Ct. (Nov. 9, 1993).

Harrison, P. J., Downes, J., & Williams, M. D. (1991). Date and acquaintance rape: Perceptions and attitude change strategies. *Journal of College Student Development, 32,* 131–139.

Haugaard, J. J., & Reppucci, N. D. (1988). *The sexual abuse of children: A comprehensive guide to current knowledge and intervention strategies.* San Francisco: Jossey-Bass.

Henneberger, M. (1994, April 27). In the young, signs that feminism lives. *The New York Times*, pp. B1, B2.

Higginson, N. (1993, November). Addressing sexual harassment in the classroom. *Educational Leadership, 51*(3), 93–96.

Higher Education Coordinating Board and Office of the Attorney General, Minnesota. (1993). *Review and comment on campus plans to prevent violence and sexual harassment*. St. Paul, MN: Author.

Hoffman, F. L. (1986). Sexual harassment in academia: Feminist theory and institutional practice. *Harvard Educational Review, 56*(2), 105–121.

Hoffman, J. (1994, January 29). Columbia U. may be sued in sex case. *The New York Times*, p. B23.

The Hotchkiss School. (1993). *Harassment policy*. Lakeville, CT: Author.

Howard v. Board of Education of Sycamore Community Unit School District # 427, 1995 WL 444147 (N.D. Ill. July 21, 1995).

Howard, M., & McCabe, J. B. (1990). Helping teenagers postpone sexual involvement. *Family Planning Perspectives, 22*(1), 21–26.

Johnson, J. D., & Russ, I. (1989). Effects of salience of consciousness-raising information on perceptions of acquaintance versus stranger rape. *Journal of Applied Social Psychology, 19*(14), 1182–1197.

Kadiki v. Virginia Commonwealth University, 1995 U.S. Dist. LEXIS 9077 (E.D. Va. June 23, 1995).

Kanter, R. M. (1977). *Men and women of the corporation*. New York: Basic Books.

Karibian v. Columbia, No. 93-7188 (2nd Cir. 1994) LEXIS 1317.

Kilborn, P. T. (1995, June 16). A leg up on ladder, but still far from top. *The New York Times*, pp. A2, A22.

Kim, M. S., & Hunter, J. E. (1993). Attitude–behavior relations: A meta-analysis of attitudinal relevance and topic. *Journal of Communication, 43*(1), 101–142.

Klein, F., & Wilber, N. (1986). *Who's hurt and who's liable: Sexual harassment in Massachusetts schools. A curriculum and guide for school personnel* (rev.). (Report No. CG 022 372). Quincy: Massachusetts State Department of Education. (Eric Document Reproduction Service No. ED 316 821)

Korf v. Ball State, 726 F.2d 1222 (7th Cir. 1984).

Koss, M. P., Gidycz, C. A., & Wisniewski, N. (1987). The scope of rape: Incidence and prevalence of sexual aggression and victimization in a national sample of higher education students. *Journal of Consulting and Clinical Psychology, 55*(2), 162–170.

LaFontaine, E., & Tredeu, L. (1986). The frequency, sources, and correlates of sexual harassment among women in traditional male occupations. *Sex Roles, 15*(7/8), 433–442.

Lee, L. A. (1987). Rape prevention: Experiential training for men. *Journal of Counseling and Development, 66*, 100–101.

Leija v. Canutillo Independent School District, 887 F. Supp. 947 (W.D. Tex. June 6, 1995).

Lenihan, G. O., Rawlins, M. E., Eberly, C. G., Buckley, B., & Masters, B. (1992).

Gender differences in rape supportive attitudes before and after a date rape education intervention. *Journal of College Student Development, 33*, 331–338.

Lewin, T. (1995, June 26). Students use law on discrimination in sex-abuse suits. *The New York Times*, pp. A1, A13.

Lindsay, D. S. (1995). Beyond backlash: Comments on Enns, McNeilly, Corkery, and Gilbert. *The Counseling Psychologist, 23*(2), 280–289.

Lipsett v. University of Puerto Rico, 864 F.20 881 (1st Cir. 1988).

Lyle v. Independent School District #709, File D341-GSS5-6N, Minnesota Department of Human Rights, Minneapolis, MN (Sept. 18, 1991).

Mamet, D. (1993). *Oleanna*. New York: Vintage Books.

Man wins harassment suit against man. (1995, August 13). *The New York Times*, p. 15.

Matthews, A. (1993, March 7). The campus crime wave. *New York Times Magazine*, pp. 38–42, 47.

McCormick, N., Adams-Bohley, S., Peterson, S., & Gaeddert, W. (1989, Fall). Sexual harassment of students at a small college. *Initiatives, 52*(3), 15–23.

Mennone v. Gordon, 889 F. Supp. 53 (D. Conn. June 15, 1995).

Meritor Savings Bank v. Vinson, 477 U.S. 57, 91 L.Ed.2d 49, 106 S.Ct. 2399 (1986).

Miller, E. (1993, July/August). Sexual harassment: Lisa's complaint. *The Harvard Education Letter*, p. 5.

Minnesota Department of Education. (1993). *It's not fun, it's illegal: The identification and prevention of sexual harassment to teenagers: A curriculum*. St. Paul, MN: Author.

Minuteman Science–Technology High School. (1993). *Guidelines for recognizing and dealing with sexual harassment* (issued November 6, 1980 and revised June 17, 1993). Lexington, MA: Author.

Modesto City Schools, 09-93-1319, December 6, 1993.

Moire v. Temple University School of Medicine, 613 F. Supp. 1360 (E.D. Pa. 1985), *aff'd*, 800 F.2d 1136 (3d Cir. 1986).

Moore, L. A., Waguespack, A. M., Wickstrom, K. F., Witt, J. C., & Gaydos, G. R. (1994). Mystery motivator: An effective and time efficient intervention. *School Psychology Review, 23*(1), 106–118.

Murduch, M., & Nichol, K. L. (1995). Women veterans' experiences with domestic violence and with sexual harassment while in the military. *Archives of Family Medicine, 4*(5), 411–418.

Murray v. New York University College of Dentistry, No. 94-9085 (2nd Cir., June 16, 1995).

Murrell, A. J., & Dietz-Uhler, B. L. (1993). Gender identity and adversarial sexual beliefs as predictors of attitudes toward sexual harassment. *Psychology of Women Quarterly, 17*, 169–175.

National Association of Scholars. (1994). *Sexual harassment and academic freedom* [Advertisement]. Princeton, NJ: Author.

National Center for Educational Statistics. (1994). *Digest of education statistics*. Washington, DC: U.S. Department of Education.

National Center for Missing and Exploited Children. (1993, May). *Selected state legislation: A guide for effective state laws to protect children.*

National Council for Research on Women. (1992). *Sexual harassment: Research and resources.* New York: Author.

New Haven Board of Education. (1994). *Sexual harassment policy and procedure.* New Haven, CT: Author.

New Jersey Department of Education. (1977). New Jersey administrative code regulations governing school desegregation 6:4-1.6, employment/contract practices, effective 1975, revised 1977.

New York State Governor's Task Force on Sexual Harassment. (1993, December). *Sexual harassment: Building a consensus for change.* Albany, NY: Author.

Newark Unified School District (Calif.), Region IX, No. 9-93-1113, July 7, 1993.

Office for Civil Rights. (1981). *Sexual harassment: It's not academic.* Washington, DC: U.S. Department of Education.

Office for Civil Rights. (1987). *Title IX grievance procedures: An introductory manual.* Washington, DC: U.S. Department of Education.

Office for Civil Rights. (1994). Unpublished raw data.

Oona R.-S. v. Santa Rosa City Schools, 890 F. Supp. 1452 (N.D. Cal. May 2, 1995).

Oregon Episcopal School. (1992). *Abuse/Sexual harassment.* Portland, OR: Author.

Paludi, M. A. (Ed.). (1990). *Ivory power: Sexual harassment on campus.* Albany: State University of New York Press.

Paludi, M. A., & Barickman, R. B. (Eds.). (1991). *Academic and workplace sexual harassment: A resource manual.* Albany: State University of New York Press.

Parrot, A. (1991, October 7). *Improving the quality of life at Cornell: A presentation on sexism, sexual harassment, and acquaintance rape.* Panel discussion, President's Council of Cornell Women, New York.

Pomerleau, A., Bolduc, D., Malcuit, G., & Cossette, L. (1990). Pink or blue: Environmental gender stereotypes in the first two years of life. *Sex Roles, 22*(5/6), 359–367.

Pope, K. S. (1993). Licensing disciplinary actions for psychologists who have been sexually involved with a client: Some information about offenders. *Professional Psychology Research and Practice, 24*(3), 374–377.

Pryor, J. B. (1987). Sexual harassment proclivities in men. *Sex Roles, 17*(5/6), 269–290.

Pryor, J. B., La Vite, C. M., & Stoller, L. M. (1993). A social psychological analysis of sexual harassment: The person/situation interaction. *Journal of Vocational Behavior, 42,* 68–83.

Purcell, P., & Stewart, L. (1990). Dick and Jane in 1989. *Sex Roles, 22*(3/4), 177–185.

Ridgewood Board of Education. (1995). *Educational administration: Sexual harassment* (issued 1988 and revised 1995). Ridgewood, NJ: Author.

Riger, S. (1991). Gender dilemmas in sexual harassment policies and procedures. *American Psychologist, 46,* 497–505.

Rimer, S. (1993, December 8). Gay rights law for schools advances in Massachusetts. *The New York Times*, p. A18.

Robertson, C., Dyer, C. E., & Campbell, D. A. (1988). Campus harassment: Sexual harassment policies and procedures at institutions of higher learning. *Signs: Journal of Women in Culture and Society, 13*, 792–812.

Roiphe, K. (1993). *The morning after: Sex, fear, and feminism on campus.* Boston: Little, Brown.

Rosa H. v. San Elizario Independent School District, 887 F. Supp. 140 (W.D. Tex. 1995).

Roscoe, B., Strouse, J. S., & Goodwin, M. P. (1994). Sexual harassment: Early adolescents' self-reports of experiences and acceptance. *Adolescence, 29*(115), 515–523.

Rosenthal, E. H., Heesacker, M., & Neimeyer, G. J. (1995). Changing the rape supportive attitudes of traditional and non-traditional male and female college students. *Journal of Counseling Psychology, 42*(2), 171–177.

Rothstein, M. (1992, September 9). More than dances and picnics greet freshmen: Orientation at Columbia includes forums on tolerance, free speech and date rape. *The New York Times*, pp. B1, B4.

Rowe, M. (1996). Dealing with harassment: A systems approach. In M. S. Stockdale (Ed.), *Sexual harassment in the workplace* (pp. 241–271). Thousand Oaks, CA: Sage.

Sadker, M., & Sadker, D. (1982). *Sex equity: Handbook for schools.* New York: Longman.

Sadker, M., & Sadker, D. (1994). *Failing at fairness: How America's schools cheat girls.* New York: Scribner's.

Sadker, M., Sadker, D., & Shakeshaft, C. (1987). Sex, sexism, and preparation of educators. *Peabody Journal of Education, 64*(4), 213–224.

Sandberg, G., Jackson, T. L., & Petretic-Jackson, P. (1987). College students' attitudes regarding sexual coercion and aggression: Developing educational and preventive strategies. *Journal of College Student Personnel, 28*, 302–311.

Sandroff, R. (1992, June). Sexual harassment: The inside story. *Working Woman*, pp. 47, 49, 50, 51, 78.

Sapon-Shevin, M., & Goodman, J. (1992). Learning to be the opposite sex: Sexuality education and sexual scripting in early adolescence. In J. T. Sears (Ed.), *Sexuality and the curriculum: The politics and practices of sexuality education* (pp. 89–105). New York: Teachers College Press.

Schmitt, E. (1994, May 1). Air force academy zooms in on sex cases. *The New York Times*, pp. A1, A34.

Schonfeld, D. J., O Hare, L. L., Perrin, E. C., Quackenbush, M., Showalter, D. R., & Cicchetti, D. V. (1995). A randomized, controlled trial of a school-based, multi-faceted AIDS education program in the elementary grades: The impact on comprehension, knowledge and fears. *Pediatrics, 95*(4), 480–486.

Scott, K. P. (1982). Sex-fair education and the male experience. *Social Education, 46*, 53–57.

Seamons v. Snow, No. 94-NC-4B (D. Utah Oct. 4, 1994).

Sexual harassment suits on the rise. (1994). *Workplace America, 1*(1), 5.

Shakeshaft, C., & Cohan, A. (1995, March). Sexual abuse of students by school personnel. *Phi Delta Kappan, 76*(7), 513-520.

Shoop, R. J., & Hayhow, J. W. (1994). *Sexual harassment in our schools.* Needham Heights, MA: Allyn & Bacon.

Siegel, D. L. (1991). *Sexual harassment: Research and resources.* New York: National Council for Research on Women.

Sprung, B. (1992). *Learning about family life: Resources for learning and teaching.* New Brunswick, NJ: Rutgers University Press.

Stanford University. (1995). *Understanding Stanford's sexual harassment policy.* Stanford, CT: Author.

State University of New York at Albany. (1991). *Policy on sexual harassment* (issued January 1981 and revised February 1991). Albany, NY: Author.

Stein, N. (1995). Sexual harassment in the school: The public performance of gendered violence. *Harvard Educational Review, 65*(2), 145-162.

Stein, N. D., Marshall, N. L., & Tropp, L. R. (1993). *Secrets in public: Sexual harassment in our schools.* Wellesley, MA: Wellesley College, Center for Research on Women.

Stein, N., & Sjostrom, L. (1994). *Flirting or hurting?: A teacher's guide on student-to-student sexual harassment in schools* (grades 6-12). Washington, DC: National Education Association and Wellesley College, Center for Research on Women.

Stoneking v. Bradford Area School District, 110 S.Ct. 840 (1992).

Strauss, S. (1988, March). Sexual harassment in the school: Legal implications for principals. *NASSP Bulletin,* pp. 93-97.

Strauss, S., & Espeland, P. (1992). *Sexual harassment and teens: A program for positive change.* Minneapolis, MN: Free Spirit.

Stringer, D. M., Remick, H., Salisbury, J., & Ginorio, A. B. (1990). The power and reasons behind sexual harassment: An employer's guide to solutions. *Public Personnel Management, 19*(1), 43-52.

Strock-Lynskey, D. (1993, October). *Prevention and historical perspective.* Speech presented at the Conference on Sexual Harassment, Teachers College, Columbia University, New York.

Strock-Lynskey, D., & Fuchs, J. E. (1987). *Sexual harassment: A digest of landmark and other significant cases.* Londonville, NY: Center for Women in Government.

Sullivan, R. (1995, June 8). Aide at high school is held in sexual abuse of a student. *The New York Times,* p. B8 .

Tangri, S. S., Burt, M. R., & Johnson, L. B. (1982). Sexual harassment at work: Three explanatory models. *Journal of Social Issues, 38*(4), 33-54.

Tangri, S. S., & Hayes, S. M. (1996). Theories of sexual harassment. In W. O'Donohue (Ed.), *Sexual harassment: Theory, research, and treatment.* Needham Heights, MA: Allyn & Bacon.

Tannen, D. (1994). *Talking from 9 to 5: Women and men in the workplace: Language, sex and power.* New York: Avon Books.

Teachers College, Columbia University. (1992, July). *Sexual harassment policy* (issued November 1989 and revised February 1992). New York: Author.

Three New York students win Westinghouse science awards. (1994, March 15). *The New York Times*, p. B3.

Till, F. J. (1980). *Sexual harassment: A report on the sexual harassment of students*. Washington, DC: National Advisory Council on Women's Educational Programs.

Title VII of the Civil Rights Act of 1964, 42 U.S.C. § 2000e et seq. (1982).

Title IX of the Education Amendments of 1972, 20 U.S.C. §§ 1681–1686 (1982).

U.S. Department of Education. (1993). *Sexual harassment: Complaints filed of incidents in U.S. Schools*.

U.S. Merit Systems Protection Board. (1981). *Sexual harassment in the federal workplace: Is it a problem?* Washington, DC: U.S. Government Printing Office.

U.S. Merit Systems Protection Board. (1988). *Sexual harassment in the federal government: An update*. Washington, DC: U.S. Government Printing Office.

The University of Iowa. (1986). *The University of Iowa policy on sexual harassment and consensual relationships*. Iowa City: Author.

The University of the State of New York. (1993). *Policy on sexual harassment*. Albany, NY: Author.

Vandell, K. (1989). *Equitable treatment of girls and boys in the classroom*. Washington, DC: American Association of University Women.

Vaux, A. (1993). Paradigmatic assumptions in sexual harassment research: Being guided without being misled. *Journal of Vocational Behavior, 42*, 116–135.

Visser, A. P., & Van Bilsen, P. (1994). Effectiveness of sex education provided to adolescents. *Patient Education and Counseling, 23*, 147–160.

Webster's New World Dictionary. (1974). Cleveland, OH: William Collins and World.

Weigel, R. H., Weiser, P. L., & Cook, S.W. (1975). The impact of cooperative learning experiences on cross-ethnic relations and attitudes. *Journal of Social Issues, 31*(1), 219–244.

Wetherfield, A. (1990). Sexual harassment: The current state of the law governing educational institutions. *Initiatives, 52*(4), 23–27.

Widoff, M. (1989). *There's no place like home . . . for sex education*. Eugene, OR: Planned Parenthood Association of Lane County.

Wilson, P., & Kirby, D. (1984). *Sexuality education: A curriculum for adolescents*. Santa Cruz: Network Publications.

Wilson, R. (1995, June 9). William and Mary seeks to shift liability for damages to professor in federal sexual harassment case. *Chronicle of Higher Education*, p. A20.

Wisconsin Department of Public Instruction. (1993). *Classroom activities in sex equity for developmental guidance*. Milwaukee: Author.

Wishnietsky, D. H. (1991). Reported and unreported teacher–student sexual harassment. *Journal of Educational Research, 84*(3), 164–169.

Woerner, W. L., & Oswald, S. L. (1993). Sexual harassment in the workplace: A view through the eyes of the courts. In E. Wall (Ed.), *Sexual harassment: Confrontations and decisions* (pp. 171–182). Buffalo, NY: Prometheus.

Yale College. (1979–1995a). *Grievance procedure for complaints of sexual harassment* (revised May 1980, April 1981, and March 1995). New Haven, CT: Author.

Yale College. (1979–1995b). *Report of the Dean's Advisory Committee on Grievance Procedure* (revised May 1980, April 1981, and March 1995). New Haven, CT: Author.

Zalk, S. R. (1990). Men in the academy: A psychological profile of harassment. In M. A. Paludi (Ed.), *Ivory power: Sexual harassment on campus* (pp. 141–176). Albany: State University of New York Press.

ADDITIONAL REFERENCES

Biklen, S. K., & Pollard, D. (Eds.). (1993). *Gender and education.* Chicago: National Society for the Study of Education.

Carroll, C. M. (1993, Winter). Sexual harassment on campus: Enhancing awareness and promoting change. *Educational Record,* pp. 21–26.

Hughes, J. O'G., & Sandler, B. R. (1988). *Peer harassment: Hassles for women on campus* (Report No. HE 021 919). Washington, DC: Association of American Colleges. (ERIC Document Reproduction Service No. ED 299 925)

Klein, S. S. (Ed.). (1985). *Handbook for achieving sex equity through education.* Baltimore: Johns Hopkins University Press.

Lyman, N. S. (1994). *Sexual harassment in American secondary schools.* Dallas: Contemporary Research Press.

Powell, E. (1991). *Talking back to sexual pressure.* Minneapolis: CompCare.

Riggs, R. O., Murrell, P. H., & Cutting, J. C. (1993). *Sexual harassment in higher education: From conflict to community* (ASHE–ERIC Higher Education Report No. 2). Washington, DC: George Washington University, School of Education and Human Development.

Rubin, L. J., & Borgers, S. B. (1990). Sexual harassment in universities during the 1980s. *Sex Roles, 23,* 397–411.

Schniedewind, N., & Davidson, E. (1993). *Open minds to equality.* Boston: Allyn & Bacon.

Sears, J. T. (1992). *Sexuality and the curriculum: The politics and practices of sexuality education.* New York: Teachers College Press.

Index

Adams, J. W., 12, 15, 19
Adams-Bohley, S., 84
Administrators
  in case studies of sexual harassment, 77–
    78
  education to prevent sexual harassment,
    90
African Americans, and sexual harassment,
  45–46
Air Force Academy, 85–86
Ajzen, I., 69, 71, 72
Alcohol, 12
Alexander v. *Yale University*, 20, 24
American Association of University Profes-
  sors (AAUP), 25, 56, 60–61, 127
American Association of University
  Women (AAUW), xv, 8, 12, 19, 43–
  45, 66, 73, 92, 94, 127–128
American Council on Education (ACE),
  140–141
American Federation of Teachers (AFT),
  128
American Psychological Association, 5, 90,
  128
Anderton, D. L., 12
Annese, J., 58
Antioch College, 84–85
Asian Americans, and sexual harassment,
  46
Assistant principals, in case studies of sex-
  ual harassment, 77–78
Aurelia D. v. *Monroe County Board of Ed-
  ucation*, 31

Bailey, N., 13, 15, 40
Baker, E., 70
Ball State, 25
Banks, J. A., 69
Barickman, R. B., xv
Barnard, W. A., 69
Beauvais, K., 71

Bell, S. T., 41
Bem, D. J., 69, 71
Benn, M. S., 69
Benson, D. J., 6, 12, 15, 19, 40
Benson, K., 7, 41
Berkowitz, A., 12
Blaming the victim, 89
Board of Cooperative Educational Services
  of Nassau County, 62
Bogart, K., 5
Bohmer, C., 9, 84
Bolduc, D., 42, 94
Botvin, E. M., 70
Botvin, G. J., 70
Bourque, L. B., 10
Brandenburg, J. B., xvii, 11, 33n., 51, 53,
  54, 55, 57, 63n., 63–64, 83, 91n.
Bridges, J. S., 42
Briere, J., 41
Brown, W. A., 12, 16, 19
Buckley, B., 70
Bundy v. *Jackson*, 28
Burt, M. R., 40, 41
Byrnes, D. A., 69

Calder, B. J., 69, 71, 72
California, 30–31, 50, 104–105, 143
Campbell, D. A., 50, 55
Cannon v. *University of Chicago*, 20, 23
Carr, R. A., 40, 71
Celis, W., 85
Center for Family Life Education, 96, 129
Center for Research on Women, 129
Center for Women Policy Studies, 129–
  130
Charlton, C., 12
Check, J. V. P., 41, 42
Child Abuse Prevention and Treatment Act
  of 1974 (P.L. 93-247), 10
Child sexual abuse
  defined, 10

Child sexual abuse (*Cont.*)
hidden or delayed memory of, 62–63
in schools, 10–11
as sexual harassment, 100–101
Cicchetti, D. V., 69, 70
City University of New York, 139
Civil Rights Act of 1871, 22
Civil Rights Act of 1964, Title VII, 1, 8, 9,
20, 22–23, 29, 49, 103
Civil Rights Act of 1991, 23
Civil Rights Restoration Act of 1987, 23
Cleveland, J. N., 40
Coaches, in case studies of sexual harassment, 81
Cohan, A., 9–12, 17, 49, 50, 62
College of William and Mary, 27
Colleges and universities. *See also specific*
schools
case studies of sexual harassment in, 78–
82
education to prevent sexual harassment
in, 68, 83–92, 139–142
legal responsibilities of, 20–21, 23, 24–
28
off-campus programs and activities, 33–
37, 63–64, 100
research on sexual harassment in, 15–16
resources for, 139–142
schools of education, 68, 86–92, 124–
125
sexual harassment grievance procedures
of, 50–51, 52–64, 118–125
sexual harassment policies of, 50–52,
118–125
Columbia University, 8, 20, 26–27, 68, 85,
89, 124–125, 142
Community, impact on sexual harassment,
42–43
Confidentiality, in grievance procedures,
54, 58–60, 99
Consensual relationships, policies concerning, 52
Contrapower harassment, 6–7, 29
Cook, S. W., 69
Corkery, J. M., 63
Cornell University, 11, 58, 70, 141, 145
Cortines, R., 11
Cossette, L., 42, 94
Counselors
in case studies of sexual harassment, 79–
80

education to prevent sexual harassment,
88–90
Crull, P., xv

Date rape, 70
Davis, D. M., 43
DeFour, D. C., 46
De Gaston, J. F., 70, 72
Del Laboratories, 6
Desegregation Assistance Centers (DACs),
149–152
DeSpelder, L. A., 69
Dey, E. L., 13, 15, 46
Diaz, T., 70
Dietz-Uhler, B. L., 41
Doe v. *Petaluma City School District*, 25–
26, 30
Douglas, W., 20
Downes, J., 70, 71
Dugenbury, L., 70
Dyer, C. E., 50, 55
Dziech, B. W., 12, 13

East Side Union High School District, 32
Eaton, S., 30
Eberly, C. G., 70
Eden Prairie, Minnesota, 29–30
Educational Equity Concepts, Inc. (EEC),
130
Educational strategies, 66–96, 97
case studies as, 73–82
in colleges and universities, 68, 83–92
components of educational intervention
on sexual harassment, 71–73
implementation of, 68–71
in K–12 schools, 92–95
model environment, 67–68
for parents, 95–96
in schools of education, 68, 86–92
Education Amendments of 1972, Title IX, 1–
2, 8, 9, 18, 20, 23–24, 25–26, 29, 30,
31, 32, 37, 49, 65, 98, 103, 147–149
Educators Guide to Controlling Sexual Harassment (EGCSH), 25, 26, 30, 32
Enns, C. Z., 63
Equal Employment Opportunity Commission (EEOC), 1–3, 6, 18, 23, 28, 33,
34, 49, 66–67
Guidelines, 23, 24, 36
Equal Protection Clause, Fourteenth
Amendment, 21–22

Eskenazi, M., 8
Espeland, P., 68
Ethnicity, and sexual harassment, 45–46

Failing at Fairness (Sadker & Sadker), 43
Fain, T. C., 12
Fair Lawn High School, 92
Family, impact on sexual harassment, 42–
    43
Family Educational Rights and Privacy Act
    of 1974 (FERPA), 152–153
Festinger, L., 69, 71
Fishbein, M., 69, 71, 72
Fitzgerald, L. F., 11, 13, 15, 40, 68
Flirting, sexual harassment versus, 98–99
Fogelson-Turet, K., 41
Fourteenth Amendment, Equal Protection
    Clause, 21–22
Franklin v. *Gwinnett County Public
    Schools*, 25
Fraternities, 12
Fried, J. P., xvi
Froschl, M., 94
Fuchs, J. E., 45
Furuto, D. M., 69
Furuto, S. B. C. L., 69
FUTURE (Females Unifying Teens to Under-
    take Responsible Education), 93

Gaeddert, W., 84
Gallen, D., 8
Gannon, L. J., 71
Garner, H., 5
Gay bashing, 8–9, 101
Gaydos, G. R., 70, 72
Gender harassment, 7–8
Gender inequity
    racial and ethnic, 45–46
    teachers and, 43–44, 88, 94–95
Gidycz, C. A., 10
Gilbert, B. J., 71
Gilbert, M. S., 63
Ginorio, A. B., 40, 45
Gold, Y., 13, 15, 40
Goldberg, C., 6, 11
Goodhart, F., 12
Goodman, J., 43
Goodwin, M. P., 17, 84
Greenhouse, L., 29
Grievance Board Model, 54
Grievance Officer Model, 53–54, 99

Grievance procedures, 49, 52–64, 98
    components of, 56–57
    confidentiality in, 54, 58–60, 99
    dilemmas concerning, 57–58
    due process versus collegial mediation
        in, 60–62
    false accusations in, 62–63
    at individual schools, 114–125
    at local level, 108–113
    models for, 53–54
    for off-campus programs and activities,
        63–64
    rights of individual versus responsibility
        of school, 58–59
    stages of, 55–56
Gross, J., 43, 69, 85
Group residences, 12
Gruber, J. E., 13
*Guidelines on Discrimination Because of
    Sex* (EEOC), 23, 24, 36
Gutek, B. A., xv, 6, 11, 14, 19, 40, 41

Hall, R., 44
Hanisch, K. A., xv
Harassment. *See also* Sexual harassment
    based on sexual orientation, 8–9, 46–47,
        101
    gender, 7–8
    repetition of, 4–5, 59–60
Harrison, P. J., 70, 71
Harris v. *Forklift Systems, Inc.*, 29
Haugaard, J. J., 10
Hayes, S. M., 6
Hayhow, J. W., xv, 66
Heesacker, M., 71
Henneberger, M., 92–93
Higginson, N., 93–94
Hoffman, F. L., 49
Hoffman, J., 20
Hofstra University, 141
Hostile environment harassment, 26–29
    cases and administrative procedures, 24,
        26–27
    defined, 3–4
    in off-campus programs and activities,
        34
    power in, 6
    prevention of, 101
    responsibility of school to provide, 58–
        59
    schools and, 51

Hotchkiss School (Connecticut), 52, 117–118
Howard, M., 69, 70, 96
Howard v. Board of Education of Sycamore Community Unit School District #427, 29
Hunter, J. E., 69

Illinois, 30
Independent Life and Accident Insurance Company, 12

Jackson, T. L., 41, 71, 90
Jensen, L., 70, 72
Johns Hopkins University, 141
Johnson, J. D., 71
Johnson, L. B., 40
Judge, T., 41

Kadiki v. Virginia Commonwealth University, 27–28
Kanter, R. M., 12
Karibian v. Columbia University, 20, 26–27
Kauppinen-Toropainen, K., 13
Kerst, J. N., 40
Kiger, G., 69
Kilborn, P. T., 70
Kim, M. S., 69
Kirby, D., 69
Korf v. Ball State, 25
Korn, J., 13, 15, 46
Koss, M. P., xv, 10
Kottke, J. L., 12, 15, 19
K–12 schools
    case studies of sexual harassment in, 74–78
    education to prevent sexual harassment in, 70, 92–95, 133–139
    incidence of sexual harassment in, 10–11
    legal responsibilities of, 25–28, 29–32, 33–36
    off-campus programs and activities of, 33–36, 63–64, 100
    research on sexual harassment in, 16–17
    resources for, 133–139
    sexual harassment grievance procedures in, 50, 52–64, 114–118
    sexual harassment policies in, 50, 51–52, 114–118
Kuriloff, P. J., 41

LaFontaine, E., 49
Latinos, and sexual harassment, 46
La Vite, C. M., 40
Lee, L. A., 71
Leija v. Canutillo Independent School District, 9, 28
Lenihan, G. O., 70
Lewin, T., 83
Lindsay, D. S., 63
Lipman, R., 6
Lipsett v. University of Puerto Rico, 21, 36
Lottes, I., 41
Lyle v. Independent School District #709, 30

Maestro-Scherer, J., 12, 16, 19
Malamuth, N. M., 41, 42
Malcuit, G., 42, 94
Mamet, D., 5
Marshall, N. L., 16, 66
Massachusetts, 8, 50, 105, 144
Massachusetts Institute of Technology, 139, 141
Masters, B., 70
Matthews, A., 12
McCabe, J. B., 69, 70, 96
McCormick, N., 84
McNeilly, C. L., 63
Mediation, 60–62
Mennone v. Gordon, 31
Meritor Savings Bank v. Vinson, 28, 45
Military, sexual harassment in, xvi, 85–86
Miller, E., 75–76
Mingle, J., 61
Minnesota, 29–30, 50, 76–77, 106, 139–140
Minuteman Science-Technology High School (Massachusetts), 116–117
Modesto City Schools, 30–31
Moire v. Temple University School of Medicine, 21, 24, 36
Moore, L. A., 70, 72
Morasch, B., 40, 41
Murduch, M., xvi, 85
Murray v. New York University College of Dentistry, 36–37
Murrell, A. J., 41
Mutziger v. Independent School District #272, 29–30

Nathanson, J., 41

National Association of Independent Schools (NAIS), 131

National Association of Scholars, 51

National Center for Educational Statistics, 48

National Center for Missing and Exploited Children, 10

National Council for Research on Women (NCRW), 13, 131

National Education Association (NEA), 131–132, 140, 144

National Organization of Women, 132

Native Americans, and sexual harassment, 46

Natural/Biological Model of sexual harassment, 40

Navy, xvi

Neimeyer, G. J., 71

Newark Unified School District, 29

New Haven, Connecticut schools, 103, 110–113

New Jersey, 29, 106–107, 113

New York City schools, 10–11, 108–110

New York State, 50, 53, 83–84, 107–108

New York State Governor's Task Force on Sexual Harassment (NYSGTF), 1, 14, 47, 50

New York University, 36–37

Nichol, K. L., xvi, 85

Off-campus programs and activities, 33–37
  cases and proceedings, 36–37
  grievance procedures for, 63–64
  responsibilities of schools and, 33–36, 100

Office for Civil Rights (OCR), 1, 2, 11–12, 18, 29, 30–31, 32, 33, 34, 49, 53, 55, 147–149

O'Hare, L. L., 69, 70

Oleanna (Mamet), 5

Oona R.-S. v. *Santa Rosa City Schools*, 31–32

Oregon Episcopal School, 114–116

Organizational Model of sexual harassment, 40

Ormerod, M., 13, 15, 40

Oswald, S. L., 28

Padgitt, J. S., 12, 15, 19

Paludi, M. A., xv, 5, 6, 40, 71, 84

Parent education
  to prevent sexual harassment, 95–96
  resources for, 142–143

Parrot, A., 9, 11, 84

Pedagogy, and sex-role stereotypes of teachers, 43–44

Peer harassment, 6–7, 98–99
  cases and administrative proceedings, 29–32
  case studies of, 75–76, 81
  same-sex, 12, 32, 101

Perrin, E. C., 69, 70

Peterson, S., 84

Petretic-Jackson, P., 41, 71, 90

Planned Parenthood, 96, 142–143

Policies, sexual harassment, 49, 51–52
  in individual schools, 114–125
  at local level, 108–113
  at state level, 104–108

Pomerleau, A., 42, 94

Pope, K. S., 90

Postponing Sexual Involvement program, 96

Power, and sexual harassment, 5–6, 11, 40–41, 46, 88

Pre-kindergarten, education programs to prevent sexual harassment in, 66, 74, 94–95

Princeton University, 141

Pryor, J. B., 40, 41, 73

Purcell, P., 43

Quackenbush, M., 69, 70

Quid pro quo harassment
  cases and administrative proceedings, 26
  defined, 2–3
  repetition of, 4

Race, and sexual harassment, 45–46

Rape
  date, 70
  defined, 10
  education programs to prevent, 70–71
  and sex-role stereotypes, 41–42
  as sexual harassment, 100–101
  statutory, 10–11

Rawlins, M. E., 70

Remick, H., 40, 45

Repetition, of harassment, 4–5, 59–60

Repp, S. E., 84

Reppucci, M. D., 10

Richards, M., 13, 15, 40
Ridgewood, New Jersey schools, 113
Riger, S., 55, 57
Rimer, S., 8
Robertson, C., 50, 55
Roiphe, K., xviii
Rosa H. v. *San Elizario Independent School District*, 21, 37
Roscoe, B., 17, 84
Rose, M., 84
Rosenthal, E. H., 71
Ross, M., 69, 71, 72
Rothstein, M., 85
Rowe, M., 55–56, 57
Russ, I., 71

Sadker, D., 43, 44, 66, 86, 88, 90, 94
Sadker, M., 43, 44, 66, 86, 88, 90, 94
St. Cloud State University, 85
St. Johns University, xvi
Salisbury, J., 40, 45
Sandberg, G., 41, 71, 90
Sandler, B., 44
Sandroff, R., 13, 15
Sapon-Shevin, M., 43
Sax, L. J., 13, 15, 46
Schmitt, E., 86
Schonfeld, D. J., 69, 70
Schools of education
  educational strategies in, 68, 86–92
  sample policies and procedures, 124–125
  working with other institutions, 91–92
Scott, K. P., 43
Seamons v. *Snow*, 32
Self-esteem, 44
Sex-role stereotypes
  in childhood, 42–43
  and gender bias, 43–44, 88, 94–95
  and rape, 41–42
Sexual assault
  defined, 9–10
  as sexual harassment, 100–101
Sexual harassment
  cases and administrative proceedings, 24–32, 36–37
  contrapower, 6–7, 29
  defined, xv, 1–2, 97
  educational strategies to prevent, 66–96, 97

effects of, xv–xvi
family and community impact on, 42–43
federal laws covering, 21–24, 152–153
flirting versus, 98–99
forms of, 7–11
grievance procedures for, 49
in higher education. *See* Colleges and universities
hostile environment, 3–4, 6, 24, 26–29, 34, 51, 58–59, 101
incidence of, 11–18
in K-12 schools. *See* K-12 schools
male, 11–12, 25
in off-campus programs and activities, 33–37, 63–64, 100
origins of, 39–48
peer, 6–7, 29–32, 75–76, 98–99, 101
policies concerning, 49, 51–52, 104–125
power and, 5–6, 11, 40–41, 46, 88
quid pro quo, 2–3, 4, 26
race and ethnicity impact on, 45–46
repetition and, 4–5, 59–60
risks and costs of bringing complaint for, 99–100
school impact on, 43–44
as sex discrimination, xvi, 3, 97
and sex-role stereotypes, 41–44
at work. *See* Workplace harassment
Sexual orientation, harassment based on, 8–9, 46–47, 101
Shakeshaft, C., 9–12, 17, 49, 50, 62, 86, 88, 90, 94
Shoop, R. J., xv, 66
Showalter, D. R., 69, 70
Shullman, S. L., 13, 15, 40, 68
Siegel, D. L., 5
Sjostrom, L., 68
Smith, M., 13
Sociocultural Model of sexual harassment, 40
South Dakota, 50
Sprung, B., 94
Stanford University, 58
State University of New York, College at Brockport, 145–146
State University of New York at Albany, 52, 121–124, 144–145
Statutory rape, 10–11

Stein, N. D., 5, 16, 31, 66, 68, 86
Stereotypes
  concerning women of color, 46
  sex-role, 41–44, 88, 94–95
Stewart, L., 43
Stoller, L. M., 40
Stoneking v. *Bradford Area School District*, 25
Strauss, S., 12, 17, 19, 68
Strickland, A. L., 69
Stringer, D. M., 40, 45
Strock-Lynskey, D., 45, 66
Strouse, J. S., 17
Student Right to Know and Campus Security Act of 1990, 153
Sullivan, R., 11, 89
Swecker, J., 13, 15, 40
Syracuse University, 142

Tanas, R., 70, 72
Tangri, S. S., 6, 40
Tannen, D., 6
Tartakovsky, F., 47–48
Teachers
  in case studies of sexual harassment, 76–78, 80–81
  education to prevent sexual harassment, 86–88, 94
  and gender bias, 43–44, 88, 94–95
  involvement in education to prevent sexual harassment, 70
Teachers College, Columbia University, 68, 89, 124–125, 142
Teaching assistants, in case studies of sexual harassment, 78–79
Teams, 12
Temple University, 21, 24, 36
There's No Place Like Home . . . for Sex Education program, 96
Thomson, G. E., 6, 12, 15, 19, 40
Till, F. J., 7
Title VII, Civil Rights Act of 1964, 1, 8, 9, 20, 22–23, 49, 103
Title IX, Education Amendments of 1972, 1–2, 8, 9, 19, 20, 23–24, 25–26, 29, 30, 31, 32, 37, 49, 65, 98, 103, 147–149
Tredeu, L., 49
Tropp, L. R., 16, 66

United Federation of Teachers (UFT), 132
U.S. Merit System Protection Board (USMSPB), 6, 13, 14, 19
University of California at Berkeley, 145
University of Chicago, 20, 23
University of Iowa, 52
University of Puerto Rico, 21, 36

Van Bilsen, P., 70
Vandell, K., 42, 43
Vaux, A., 41
Violence Against Women Act of 1994 (VAWA), 153
Virginia Commonwealth University, 27–28
Visser, A. P., 70

Waguespack, A. M., 70, 72
Washington State, 50
Weed, S. E., 70, 72
Weigel, R. H., 69
Weiner, L., 12, 13
Weiser, P. L., 69
Weitzman, L., 13, 15, 40
Westinghouse Science Talent Search, 47–48
Wetherfield, A., 22
Wickstrom, K. F., 70, 72
Widoff, M., 96
Williams, M. D., 70, 71
Wilson, P., 69
Wilson, R., 20, 27
Wisconsin, 69, 130
Wishnietsky, D. H., 10, 16, 17
Wisniewski, N., 10
Witt, J. C., 70, 72
Woerner, W. L., 28
Women's Educational Equity Act (WEEA), 133
Workplace harassment
  education to prevent, 69–70
  hostile environment, 6, 26–27, 28–29
  male-on-male, 12
  quid pro quo, 26–27
  research on, 14–15

Yale University, 20, 24, 57, 58–60, 89, 118–121

Zalk, S. R., 6, 40, 71

About the Author

Judith Berman Brandenburg is Professor of Psychology and Education at Teachers College, Columbia University. She served as Dean of Teachers College from 1985 to 1994 and was the first woman to hold that position. Here she initiated sexual harassment grievance procedures, a faculty seminar on the Scholarship on Women and Gender, grants to support faculty and student research, and worked to increase women faculty from 32% to 50% and faculty of color from 5% to 12%.

Before joining TC (1977–85) she was Associate Dean of Yale College, Yale University. There she played a leading role in establishing the Women's Studies Program and chaired a committee that developed grievance procedures for sexual harassment complaints.

Prior to Yale she was an Assistant Professor and psychologist in the Counseling Center at Queens College of CUNY, where she initiated programs for older women and open admissions students, and received a Favorite Teacher Award.

She received her B.S. degree from Cornell University, M.A.T. degree from Harvard University, and Ph.D. degree from New York University.

Much of her professional and personal life has been dedicated to equity issues and to assuring access and excellence in education.

She lives in New York City, is married to Lane H. Brandenburg, and has two sons, David and Neal.